ONE
NATION

U N D E R

GOD

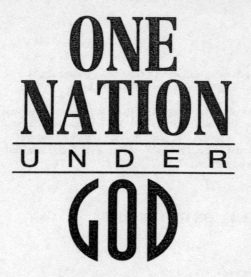

ONE
NATION
UNDER
GOD

BOB YANDIAN

Whitaker House

Unless otherwise indicated, all Scripture quotations are taken
from the *King James Version* (KJV) of the Bible.

Scripture quotations marked (AMP) are from the *Amplified New
Testament*, © 1954, 1958, 1987 by The Lockman Foundation
and used by permission; or are from the *Amplfied Bible, Old
Testament*, © 1962, 1964 by Zondervan Pubishing House, and
used by permission.

ONE NATION UNDER GOD

Bob Yandian
Bob Yandian Ministries
P.O. Box 55236
Tulsa, OK 74155

ISBN: 0-88368-359-8
Printed in the United States of America
Copyright © 1988 by Bob Yandian

Whitaker House
580 Pittsburgh Street
Springdale, PA 15144

1 2 3 4 5 6 7 8 9 10 11 / 04 03 02 01 00 99 98 97 96 95

Table of Contents

1

Blessed Is the Nation
Whose God Is the Lord

A nation's success depends upon believers in Jesus
Christ who rely and act on the Word of God as explained
in the Bible. When a nation looks at God as its leader, the
nation will succeed. Psalm 33:12 states: "Blessed is the nation
whose God is the Lord..."

We who are believers in Jesus Christ "...are the salt of
the earth..." (Matt. 5:13). We know that salt preserves and
flavors. As believers, we are the preservers of the earth (the
Greek word for "earth" — *ge* — refers to physical land) —
we are the hands, the feet, the voice of Jesus Christ on the
earth. And we are called by God to be conquerors and
victors. (Rom. 8:37; 1 Cor. 15:57.) As believers, we flavor
"bland" conditions, causing them to change.

Matthew 5:13 states: "...if the salt have lost its savour,
wherewith shall it be salted? it is thenceforth good for
nothing, but to be cast out, and to be trodden under foot
of men."

Mark 9:50 tells us that to keep from losing our "saltness"
to "...Have salt in yourselves, and have peace with one
another": to stay in God's Word and to live in forgiveness.
When we abide in Jesus and Jesus' words abide in us (John
15:7), that fellowship with the Lord is having salt in
ourselves. When we have peace with one another, we are
maintaining that fellowship — that right relationship — with
other people and God to maintain the ability to season the
world around us.

We "...are the light of the world..." (Matt. 5:14). (The Greek word for "world" — *kosmos* — refers to the world's order or the world's system.) We believers have been placed on earth by God to dispel Satan's darkness which wraps the world's system. We are the salt of the physical land we stand on, but we are the light in a world of darkness.

We are exhorted to pray for our nation and leaders: "For kings, and for all that are in authority; that we may lead a quiet and peaceable life in all godliness and honesty" (1 Tim. 2:2).

Throughout the Bible we see that God has preserved nations for a remnant, a few believers who will trust in Him. Ezekiel 22:30 states that the Word of the Lord came saying: "And I sought for *a man* among them, that should make up the hedge, and stand in the gap before me for the land, that I should not destroy it: but I found none."

In that instance, the Lord found no one. But today He can find believers who will stand in the gap and pray for the nation that it will not be destroyed.

We in America have such problems as pornography, child abuse, and sexual permissiveness due to the cause of the disease that lies behind these symptoms: as a whole, we as a nation have stopped relying upon the principles in the Bible. But in spite of our problems in America, we still exist as the strong nation we are today, because the Church of the Lord Jesus Christ has a remnant which refuses to lose its savour.

America is not a great nation because its people as a whole pray. America is great because of the salt within the nation, the remnant of the people who know the Lord God. The Bible does not say that if the *whole nation* prays, God will heal the land; it says: "If *my* people, which are called by *my* name, shall humble *themselves*, and pray, and seek my face, and turn from their wicked ways; then will I hear from heaven, and forgive their sin, and will heal their land" (2 Chron. 7:14).

Satan (referred to as "the god of this world" in 2 Cor. 4:4) has dominion and some authority as the ruler of this earth. He is the one behind the problems in our nation today. But when Jesus after being crucified rose from the dead, He gave us authority over Satan's power, and the Bible contains much instruction in how to use that power. Jesus said, ". . .I will build my church; and the gates of hell shall not prevail against it" (Matt. 16:18). He also said, ". . .Occupy till I come" (Luke 19:13).

"Occupy," a Greek military term, means to take over the land and keep it. We believers are in enemy territory. We are to take the land from the enemy, Satan; set up camp; occupy until the Lord Jesus comes — and not be trodden under foot! We are to put Satan under *our* feet. (Luke 10:19.) We also know that Satan's days are numbered, because the Bible shows us that Jesus Christ will rule and reign in the end and Satan will be imprisoned. (Rev. 19:11-16; 20:1-3.)

The Bible says in Ephesians 3:10 that God is manifesting to the principalities and powers in the heavenly places, through the Church, His manifold wisdom. We the Church are here to show the earth — the demons, Satan — God's manifold wisdom.

In the midst of a world that is crumbling, filled with problems, that knows war, we can stay together; we can bring peace to our nation. In the midst of it all, we can bring individual peace, because we are the salt of the earth.

In this book, we will study the instructions the Bible gives us in praying for a good and prosperous nation. Through hearing God's Word and through prayer, we can make the difference!

2

God Established the Nations and Ordains the Governments

Before the flood of Noah, the world was one nation: "...the whole earth was of one language, and of one speech" (Gen. 11:1). But the people tried to unite to make one nation under the heavens that man would run. They worked, striving together to build the tower of Babel. The nations as we know them today were divided when "...the Lord did there confound the language of all the earth: and from thence did the Lord scatter them abroad upon the face of all the earth" (Gen. 11:9).

God had to "scatter them abroad" because what they were doing was coming to evil. He made an amazing statement regarding the people who had become one: "...and now nothing they have imagined they can do will be impossible to them" (Gen. 11:6 AMP).

Man was made in the image of God (Gen. 1:27), but when Adam and Eve sinned and disobeyed God in the Garden of Eden, man fell, separating himself from God. (Gen. 2:16,17; 3:1-24.) Eve was tempted by Satan and ate the fruit that God had forbidden her and Adam to eat, then gave the fruit to Adam. He ate also, and sin, the nature of the flesh, entered into them. A curse entered them which spread upon all the inhabitants of the earth after them. Romans 5:12 tells us: "Wherefore, as by one man (Adam) sin entered into the world, and death by (through) sin; and so death (spiritual and physical) passed upon all men, for that all have sinned."

Today man is under a curse which came from Adam and his sin. The only way out of that curse is through the last Adam, the Lord Jesus Christ. He came to undo what the first Adam did. First Corinthians 15:22 tells us: "For as in Adam all die, even so in Christ shall all be made alive."

Adam was given a lease on this earth from God. He was told to "have dominion" and to "subdue" the earth. (Gen. 1:26,28). Instead, through disobedience, he gave the dominion to God's enemy, Satan. For the remainder of the term of the lease, Satan became the god of this world. (2 Cor. 4:4). Adam, in essence, sublet this earth to Satan. Even though man fell and now has a fallen nature, he still has — far above all the creatures of this earth — this ability within himself: what he strives for, he can attain. But because of this fallen nature, unless man aims that ability in the right direction, he will be destroyed by it. Therefore, God has a plan for man and Satan has a plan. Following Satan's plan brings momentary success, but eventual destruction. (Prov. 16:25.) God's plan brings success in life and eternity.

At the tower of Babel, God had to scatter the people so that man would not destroy himself. Although Satan is the god of this world, he is not the ruler of the universe. He may rent the apartment, but God owns the building. When Satan oversteps his boundaries, God will step in as He has done so many times in history. Even at times when it appears that this world has gone too far and evil will take over, God will not allow it to happen. Jesus witnessed the first time Satan was overthrown from heaven (Luke 10:18) and will witness the last time Satan is overthrown from the earth. (Rev. 19:11-21.) Satan's kingdom and world leaders will be destroyed at the return of Jesus. (2 Thess. 2:8,9.)

After the tower of Babel, there was a man who rose up: Abraham. Abraham had a vision of the Lord Jesus Christ, and a promise was given to him. God promised to give him two sets of offspring, called "seed." One would be as the

12

sand of the sea, a natural race of people, the Jewish people. The other set would be as the stars of heaven (Gen. 15:5), a spiritual race of people of all nations who would believe in the Lord as their savior. (Gal. 3:8,19.) The nation of Israel is the subject of God's dealings with man in the Old Testament. The principles God gave Israel for their nation to become a success are the principles God expects nations to use today.

God Established Governments —

Both in the Old and New Testaments the Bible explains our responsibilities to the government and to the government leaders of the land.

ROMANS 13:1-4

Let every soul be subject unto the higher powers. For there is no power but of God: the powers that be are ordained of God.

Whosoever therefore resisteth the power, resisteth the ordinance of God: and they that resist shall receive to themselves damnation.

For rulers are not a terror to good works, but to the evil. Wilt thou then not be afraid of the power? do that which is good, and thou shalt have praise of the same:

For he is the minister of God to thee for good . . .

God is the One Who establishes governments: He is also the One Who ordained that we should have human leadership to run those governments. Although God may not choose the man who occupies an office, the position is God ordained. How a man or woman fulfills that position will eventually be handled before God Himself. For example, Adolf Hitler was not God's choice for the office, but his position as leader of his country was ordained by God. Many people are good choices when they take over an office, but become corrupt while in that position. God will eventually remove those people from office and replace them. The individuals may come and go, but the position remains.

The Old Testament shows us an example of this in Saul, King of Israel. Although he was God's choice in the beginning, he became corrupt while in office. Samuel anointed Saul, then a few years later anointed his successor, David. Romans 13:1 says, ". . .there is no power but of" (*from*) "God: the powers that be" (*exist*) "are ordained of God."

The words *power* and *powers* are from the Greek word *exousia*. These words should be translated "authority" and "authorities." The actual meaning of this verse is that there is no authority but of God; the authorities that be, or that exist — government — are ordained of God.

Whether it is the authority in a classroom, a home, a church, a government, or in the military, all authority is designed by and comes from God, because God Himself established authority.

Even the Godhead exercises authority. God the Father is in authority over the Lord Jesus Christ, Who is in authority over the Holy Spirit. The Church is subject to the Lord Jesus Christ, and we learn authority from His Word.

Every person, both believer and unbeliever, is to be subject to the higher authorities, the government, which are ordained of God. Verse 1 begins by telling us, "Let *every* soul be subject unto the higher powers. . ."

With the breakup of the home today we actually have the breakup of the center of authority. Satan knows this. The home is really an incubator for a small child to learn about authority and carry that discipline into his later life so that the nation will not disintegrate. That is why there is such a tremendous attack today on the home.

Verse 2 says, "Whosoever therefore resisteth the power" (*authority*) "resisteth the ordinance of God: and they that resist shall receive to themselves damnation." The word *damnation* here means "judgment." It means judgment under those in authority. This could mean going to court, being fined, going to jail or prison, or capital punishment.

Verse 3 says: "For rulers are not a terror to good works, but to the evil. . ." The reason rulers are placed on earth is to protect the good and to remove the evil.

Verse 3 continues: ". . . Wilt thou then not be afraid of the power" (*authority*)? "do that which is good, and thou shalt have praise of the same. . ." If you obey the law, the same authorities which have the power to put you in prison or fine you, will praise you.

We have already seen in verse 1 that government is ordained of God. Because of this, if we rebel against government, we are rebelling against God. Rebellion, which First Samuel 15:23 calls "as the sin of witchcraft," began with Satan who rebelled against God. We identify with Satan when we rebel against the authority God put on the earth. To resist the policeman, the judge, or the teacher in the classroom is to resist God. The child rebelling against his parents is rebelling against God. The congregation member rebelling against the pastor is rebelling against God.

We may not agree with every decision a leader makes. There is not a perfect leader on earth except the Lord Jesus Himself. There is nothing wrong with *questioning* authority, but *rebellion* against authority is not allowed in God's Word. Unless a leader directly violates a scripture in the Word of God, we are to submit whether we believe the request is right or wrong or whether we like or dislike the person who made the request.

When a nation, state, or city levies taxes, establishes speed limits and puts up stop signs and traffic signals, we as believers or unbelievers are to obey the laws. We may not agree with the amount of taxes or like the posted speed limit, but we are to submit and obey. The Bible does not give us the exact amount of taxes we are to pay; whether we believe the amount is fair or unfair, we are to pay our taxes.

Throughout history, Roman taxes were high and even higher in the days of Jesus, because tax collectors took advantage of the Jews. Publicans (tax collectors) were hated in Israel because they were corrupt. (Luke 19:1-8.) Yet when Peter's taxes were due, Jesus did not tell him to forget paying them because taxes were unfair. Jesus provided the money for the taxes by telling Peter to go fishing. The first fish had enough money in its mouth to pay Peter's taxes. But, on the other hand, we are not required to obey government laws if they specifically violate God's Word.

Peter and the other apostles were submissive to the government and respected it. But when they were commanded not to teach God's Word, as ministers of God they "...answered and said, We ought to obey God rather than men" (Acts 5:29).

Verse 4 begins: "For he" (*the leader of the government*) "is the minister of God to thee for good..." The Greek word for "minister" in this verse is *diakonos*, the same Greek word that refers to a minister within the church. (1 Cor. 3:5.) Did you ever think of your mayor or president as a minister of God? God sees a government leader as a minister as much as he sees a pastor of a church as a minister. A minister of the gospel may abuse his office and treat people unfairly, but his office is of God. God will replace him with another person, but the office continues. Ministers come and go but the offices in the Body of Christ are still here today. You may agree or disagree with your pastor's decisions, but you are still to respect, submit and obey him as you do the Lord. (1 Thess. 5:12,13; Heb. 13:7,17.)

Ministers, whether in the church or government, are from God. The church is not the state and the state is not the church, but the two are still inseparable. They walk hand in hand, and therefore, should agree. (Amos 3:3.) As we will discuss in more detail in a later chapter, the purpose of the state is to provide protection, freedom and peace for the people. This provides freedom for people to choose for or against the gospel. The church is to pray for, offer counsel and spiritual guidance to the state in order to remain in line with the principles of God's Word and give the devil no place.

Both the Old and New Testaments record that prophets of God spoke up concerning government actions. Paul used the law to protect himself from being unfairly treated by the religious Pharisees. (Acts 22:24-29.) Church and state should protect each other, not abuse.

The operation of government in the earth is God-given. Without government, our nation would fall apart. God established government in order to protect its citizens and set up safeguards so that believers are able to fulfill the Great Commission and spread the gospel. (Mark 16:15-17.)

God desires that leadership look for direction from Him. He desires that we have natural men to follow after, and these men, in turn, follow after the things of God. Paul said, "Be ye followers of me, even as I also am of Christ" (1 Cor. 11:1).

Government also is a teacher to natural men of the way God runs His Kingdom. God uses natural things in this earth to teach of spiritual. He uses marriage to teach of the relationship of Jesus and His Church. (Eph. 5:23-32.) He uses the natural family to teach of the unity and love we have as children of God. (1 John 3:1.) He uses the local church to teach us of the universal invisible Church, the Body of Christ. Human government teaches us about authority and submission to God Himself. The reward and discipline system established on earth helps teach us of the consequences of rejection and rewards of acceptance of God's plan. "Behold therefore the goodness and severity of God.." (Rom. 11:22.) Therefore, government is to represent and teach of God, not to take the place of God.

Satan has tried to stop the spread of the gospel through his own plans of anarchy and totalitarian government. Satan still tries to *be* God. He will work through government if he can. This is why we are to pray for government leaders and against the prince of the power of the air. If a government turns against God, His people and His Word, it is held accountable as was Pharaoh and Nebuchadnezzar. (Exod. 8-11; Dan. 4.)

Angelic and satanic forces are fighting for control of nations. (Dan. 10:12,13; Eph. 6:12.) Both sides desire to control the leaders of governments. If a leader heeds the voice of God's Word and runs the nation accordingly, the nation will be blessed. (Ps. 33:12.) If Satan's voice is heeded, the nation is in trouble, but not necessarily without hope. The nation can be blessed because of the "salt" in the nation, the remnant of believers who hold steadfastly to God's Word, pray for their nation and exercise their rights in participating in the government system.

We have a right as American citizens and Christians to search out candidates who adhere to the principles of God's Word. Then we need to pray over the candidates and vote. We need to put actions to our prayers. "Even so faith, if it hath not works, is dead, being alone" (James 2:17). God desires leadership in a nation who knows His Word and His voice.

As we have seen so far, there are reasons why nations prosper and decline. God's Word is specific on this issue, not cloudy or unclear. A nation is not blessed or cursed because of legislation. Godly leadership and godly people ensure a nation's success. In the next chapters we will begin to look with clarity at God's instructions for a successful nation.

3

The Knowledge of God
Will Preserve the Land

We read in the New Testament that the incidents in the Old Testament are written down as examples for us. (1 Cor. 10:11.) From the instructions God gave Israel in the Old Testament, we can learn the principles which lead to the prosperity or decline of a nation. In examining the causes of a nation's decline, we can see that by applying the opposite, a nation can become great.

HOSEA 4:1-6

Hear the word of the Lord, ye children of Israel: for the Lord hath a controversy with the inhabitants of the land, because there is no truth, nor mercy, nor knowledge of God in the land.

By swearing, and lying, and killing, and stealing, and committing adultery, they break out, and blood toucheth blood.

Therefore shall the land mourn, and everyone that dwelleth therein shall languish, with the beasts of the field, and with the fowls of heaven; yea, the fishes of the sea also shall be taken away.

Yet let no man strive, nor reprove another: for thy people are as they that strive with the priest.

Therefore shalt thou fall in the day, and the prophet also shall fall with thee in the night, and I will destroy thy mother.

My people are destroyed for lack of knowledge: because thou hast rejected knowledge, I will also reject thee, that thou shalt be no priest to me: seeing thou hast forgotten the law of thy God, I will also forget thy children.

Hear the Word of the Lord —

Hosea 4:1 begins, "Hear the word of the Lord, ye children of Israel:..." The Word of the Lord by itself is not what brings a nation out of the disease it is in; it is the believers who *hear* the Word of the Lord and do it, because "...faith cometh by hearing, and hearing by the word of God" (Rom. 10:17).

It is not the truth that makes us free, it is *knowing* the truth that makes us free. Jesus said, "...If ye continue in my word, then are ye my disciples indeed; and ye shall know the truth, and the truth shall make you free" (John 8:31,32).

Disciples are people who follow after Jesus, who continue in His Word. Disciples are not only pastors, prophets, and evangelists, but housewives, mechanics, carpenters, and architects. The calling of a pastor is not more important than the calling of a housewife or a carpenter, because God has called the whole Body of Christ to win the world. He has asked students to win students and businessmen to win businessmen. Today America needs more disciples who will follow closely the Lord Jesus Christ, hear the Word of the Lord, and pray for the nation.

Verse 1 continues: "...for the Lord hath a *controversy* with the inhabitants of the land,..." When I was a little boy I knew I was in trouble when my Dad said, "I have a bone to pick with you." That meant he had a controversy with me.

I believe that America, our great nation, is blessed because of its strong Christians. But even so, God has a bone to pick with us — a controversy. America's foundations are based on Bible truths. Our founding fathers established America on Christian principles which include the right and freedom to worship God. Our documents are filled with the name of the Lord and were signed after prayer. Our early presidents were godly men who prayed during battles which purchased our nation's freedom. They attended church, and the Bible was the major textbook of the schools.

God's controversy with us is that in our nation we have left these foundations and principles. Verse 1 says the Lord has a controversy with the inhabitants of the land ". . . because there is no truth, nor mercy, nor knowledge of God in the land." The truth is God's Word. God is saying that the inhabitants have left His Word, the Bible. In the day of the Israel of Hosea, it was difficult to find the Bible being taught or applied in the everyday life of the people. Except for the prophets who were preaching of the coming of captivity, prayer and Bible study were at an all time low.

Today there is so little knowledge of Who God is. If you ask someone on the street, "Who is God?" he will probably say something like, "God is in the trees, the air, the grass, in the rocks around us. You're god, I'm god." Many people acknowledge that God exists, but do not know him. And some people have only heard the names "God" and "Jesus" used as swear words. They do not know that God is love, the great "I AM," the One whose eyes run to and fro throughout the whole earth to show Himself strong on behalf of them whose heart is perfect toward Him. (1 John 4:16; Ex. 3:14; 2 Chron. 16:9.) And they do not know that Jesus is the only way they can reach Him. (John 14:6.)

Someone may ask, "Why isn't there much knowledge of God in the land?" Because there is so little truth, so little of the Word. Where there is no Word, there is no knowledge of God. People need to understand Who God is and what His character is like. The more they understand God, the

23

more His character of love and grace becomes known to them.

In verse 1, God is saying, "You've forsaken the Word, you've forsaken mercy, and there is no knowledge of Me in the land."

When we ignore the knowledge of God, we exalt man. When we exalt man and set him up as God, we are on the road to destruction, because Satan is behind this. (Gen. 3:5.) Satan wants us to glorify man and have him look for answers from man.

The Bible tells us not to compare ourselves with other men, but with "the measure of the rule" God gives us, His Word. Those who compare themselves to others are not wise. (2 Cor. 10:12,13.) When nations compare themselves to each other rather than to the divine standard of God's Word, they decline.

Sometimes people who are doing something wrong will say, "Well, at least I'm not as bad as my neighbor." Why should your neighbor be the standard? I see standards in America lowering year by year, almost week by week. Each year the new television programs present worse standards than they did the year before. But should we say, "Well, at least we're not as bad as some other countries"?

Why should we set our standards by the standards of other countries? Other countries may be comparing themselves with America. We all need to come back to the unchanging Word of God. People may try to tell us that the Bible is outdated — that we Christians are not "with it." But, we are — we are with Him. Our standard is based on God's inspired Word and it never changes, because God never changes. (Mal. 3:6; Heb. 13:8.)

Satan Comes to Steal the Good Things God Gives —

God's controversy with America is that we as a whole have not been hearing His Word. God desires that we be

24

blessed, but He knows that when we do not listen to His Word, symptoms of disease appear in our country. When believers within a nation turn from God, they are opening the door for Satan and for military destruction to come into that nation. We see in the Bible that when a nation fell, it was militarily.

Israel resurrected from destruction a number of times. God promised to Abraham that his seed would go on forever. He promised a natural seed called the Jew that would always be here. He promised a spiritual race which would also be established forever. These are both special to God. He is jealous over them and protects them. Those who respect them will be blessed by God. Those who do not will be cursed.

He promised that those who blessed Israel would be blessed; those who cursed that nation would be cursed. (Gen. 12:3.) But Deuteronomy 28 and Leviticus 26 tell us that when Israel as a whole rejected the Lord, they would be defeated militarily (Lev. 26:27-33; Deut. 28:47-52,63,64) and taken into captivity. God would see to it that the nation would recover, but that is how serious it was for the nation to stop hearing the Word of the Lord.

Deuteronomy, chapter 28, verses 1 through 14 describe the blessings which are promised to those people who follow after the ways of the Lord. But verses 15 through 68 describe the curses which befall a nation that does not follow after the ways of the Lord.

It is very important to note that in verses 15 through 68 the Hebrew actually implies that God will have to *allow* the curses, because He cannot stop them. God is not the cause of the curse. God is the Source of blessings. He gives us spiritual and natural possessions. He gives us a country and all of its abundance. When He gives us blessings, it is not God, but Satan who wants to take them away. Disobedience opened the door for Satan to curse the Israelites while they were in the wilderness. (1 Cor. 10:1-10.)

Mark, chapter 4, the parable of the sower, tells us that when God sent the seed of the Word into the ground, Satan came to steal the seed that was sown. The key to spiritual growth in the parable is not on the part of the sower, the seed or the enemy who comes to steal, but the ground, the heart of the believer. The key verse is Mark 4:23: "If any man have ears to hear, let him hear" (*the Greek means "keep on hearing"*). If we "continue in the word," Satan cannot steal it. If we do not, we nor God can stop the devil from stealing the blessings from God, "every good and every perfect gift" (James 1:17). The second half of Deuteronomy, chapter 28, beginning with verse 15 describes what happens to the nation which does not "hearken unto the voice of the Lord thy God" (v. 2).

If we guard the Word of God in our heart, the Word will guard us. God gives us His Word, but we need to maintain that Word in us. Just as it is important that we keep God's Word in our heart and guard it, it is the same with all blessings. We need to protect, keep and guard the blessings God gives us by following after His Word and His Spirit.

**Departing from God's Word
Brings Destruction to a Nation —**

Deuteronomy 28:47 says:

Because thou servedst not the Lord thy God with joyfulness, and with gladness of heart, for the abundance of all things.

Serve the Lord Who gave you all things; do not serve the things or let things get in the way of the Giver of things.

VERSE 48

Therefore shalt thou serve thine enemies which the Lord shall send against thee, in hunger, and in thirst, and in nakedness, and in want of all things: and he shall put a yoke of iron upon thy neck, until he have destroyed thee.

This verse is not saying that God will do these things. As we discussed, God does not send you great blessings, then calamity. Satan is the one who comes ". . .to steal, and to kill, and to destroy." (John 10:10.)

VERSE 49

The Lord shall bring a nation against thee from far, from the end of the earth, as swift as the eagle flieth; a nation whose tongue thou shalt not understand.
(This is foreign military intervention.)

VERSE 50

A nation of fierce countenance, which shall not regard the person of the old, nor shew favour to the young.

We need to keep at bay those fierce nations whose leaders do not regard the life of the old or the young, in other words, whose leaders regard possessions and power above life. But if those nations attack, and we hearken to the voice of the Lord, God will give us strength to defeat them.

VERSES 51, 52

And he shall eat the fruit of thy cattle, and the fruit of thy land, until thou be destroyed: which also shall not leave thee either corn, wine, or oil, or the increase of thy kine, or flocks of thy sheep, until he have destroyed thee.

And he shall besiege thee in all thy gates, until thy high and fenced walls come down, wherein thou trustedst, throughout all thy land; and he shall besiege thee in all thy gates throughout all thy land: which the Lord thy God hath given thee.

We see throughout God's Word that when Israel left God's promises, it was attacked militarily by other nations (according to verse 49 — "whose tongue" or language — "thou shalt not understand").

Joel described that a nation was going to come into Israel in four waves as locust coming into the land to eventually totally destroy the crops of Israel. (Joel 1:4.) He drew an analogy that the Assyrian army would come in, in four waves under different leaders. He prophesied this would come to pass, because the people had left God's Word: the priests were not preaching it, the people had turned away from God and were pursuing prosperity — the *things* that God had given them — rather than *Him*.

Leviticus 26:13-39 tells us the way that the enemy comes into a nation. Chapter 26 describes cycles of judgment. When a nation begins to turn away from the Lord in rebellion, internal destruction begins to come. Each stage is progressive. There are climatic changes. The land will not yield its increase. The heavens will not give rain; the ground will dry up. I think today's worldwide environmental catastrophies stem from people having left God's Word to go their own ways.

Sickness and disease break out among the people. Next military occupation by a foreign power takes place. Finally, the nation is destroyed and dispersed.

Israel was once controlled by Babylon. After refusing to turn to the Lord, Israel was dispersed, taken captive into the nation of Babylon for seventy years while Israel's land sat desolate and empty. When Jesus came into Israel, even though Israel was still a nation, it was occupied by the military of Rome. Herod and Pilot were rulers in Rome.

Jesus preached repentance, but Israel would not repent. "He came unto his own, and his own received him not" (John 1:11). Finally Jesus stood over the city of Jerusalem and wept. He said, "O Jerusalem, Jerusalem. . .how often would I have gathered thy children together, even as a hen gathereth her chickens under her wings, and ye would not!" (Matt. 23:37). He said, ". . .Jerusalem shall be trodden down of the Gentiles, until the times of the Gentiles be fulfilled" (Luke 21:24). In 70 A.D. Israel was dispersed by the Roman armies.

After Israel was restored in 1948, the people of Israel began returning to the land. Israel went through the cycle described in Leviticus, chapter 26, twice. We can see the evidence of God's prophecies being true. All nations can put their trust in the God of Israel.

If curses begin to overtake a nation that has not adhered to the principles of the Word of the Lord, the curses can be removed through Jesus Christ. Believers must repent for their own sins of complacency and the sins of the nation. (Dan. 9:3-11). By returning to the Lord, cursing can be turned into blessing. (Is. 55:7.)

4
Stopping Crime

Even though Hosea was written thousands of years ago, God's principles taught in it still apply. The standard of God's Word will be the same one hundred years from now as it was two thousand years ago. God's Word is always right — it is the truth. And when we leave that standard, God has a controversy with us.

Hosea 4:1 gives us the cause of a disease in a nation: when a nation turns from the Word, it turns from God's blessings. And when the nation reaches the point of there being little knowledge of God in the land, the symptoms of the disease run rampant.

Verse 2 describes the symptoms: "By swearing, and lying, and killing, and stealing, and committing adultery, they break out, and blood toucheth blood." The symptoms fall into two categories. The first deals with crime: swearing, lying, stealing, and killing.

Swearing in this verse does not mean *cursing*, but refers to bad business deals: Oaths given and promises made but never kept. A person's word cannot be trusted anymore. Lying is a symptom of disease in a land. When cheating and false oaths in business are acceptable, and people do not stick by their word, these are outward symptoms of inward rebellion against the standard of God's Word. Other symptoms will soon manifest: lying, killing, stealing and committing adultery. In this verse *stealing* refers to theft, armed robbery, and looting running rampant in the land.

Killing in this verse means "murder." Statistics in the media tell us crime in this country has become worse through the years. Our government has passed crime legislation to try to control it and formed commissions on crime trying to find the causes. Sometimes the environment in which people grow up is blamed. But it is not the environment *outside* that is important, it is the atmosphere *inside* people that is important. They need to receive Jesus as Lord and have God's Word abide in them. Our country could save the millions of dollars spent studying crime by just going to God's Word.

Genesis, chapter 4, describes the first criminal, Cain. He had a knowledge of God's Word, but did not use it.

Cain and Abel were the first sons born to Adam and Eve. After Adam and Eve sinned, the Lord taught them how to obtain remission of sins through the shedding of blood. Adam and Eve must have passed the ways of sacrifice on to Cain and Abel.

Abel offered an acceptable sacrifice to the Lord of a lamb. It was "the firstlings of his flock," the finest. (v. 4.) Then of the finest, Abel brought the finest parts of the lamb to sacrifice to the Lord, because the Lord was looking for the blood.

Cain, however, came in his own pride and gave of his own works to the Lord: the fruit of the ground, a bloodless sacrifice — a sacrifice not pleasing to the Lord. Cain probably had the biggest of everything to offer the Lord, but when he offered it and the Lord refused it, Cain became angry.

Cain had knowledge of the proper ways, but did not use it. Hosea 4:6 states: "My people are destroyed for lack of knowledge..." but goes on to say that God's people have had the knowledge — they know what to do — but are just not using it: "because thou hast rejected knowledge..."

Today some of America's problems result from there being little knowledge of God in the land. Others result from there being knowledge of God's Word in the land, but it not being used.

God offered Cain another opportunity. He said, "If thou doest well, shalt thou not be accepted?..." (Gen. 4:7). He was saying, "You found out I did not accept this offering, but you still have an opportunity to do as Abel your brother and bring the right offering."

But because Cain was so puffed up in pride, he took his anger out on Abel and killed him. (Cain must have learned how to kill by watching Abel sacrifice the lamb.)

Cain was the first murderer. But he also lied. When God asked Cain where Abel was, Cain said he did not know. He tried to cover up his crime. He said, "Am I my brother's keeper?" (v. 9). In other words Cain was saying, "Why are you asking me? Doesn't my brother have a right to privacy; don't I have a right to privacy?"

There are certain divine laws or rights that God wants all people to have. One of them is a right to privacy. God has given every believer that right and a nation should protect it.

First Peter 4:15 says, "But let none of you suffer as a murderer, or as a thief, or as an evildoer, or as a busybody in other men's matters." In other words each man has a right to his own privacy. You can choose where you live, have as many kids as you want, and do whatever you want, unless it invades somebody else's privacy. But notice that if you gossip about or judge somebody, you are invading his privacy; in fact, Jesus said, "Whosoever hateth his brother is a murderer" (1 John 3:15). Busybodying, talking about people, and judging them can be the same as murdering them and we can figure out really quick that murder is invading somebody's privacy.

But in the example of Cain and Abel, notice that Cain pleaded privacy: "Am I my brother's keeper?" Cain had already violated Abel's privacy and he was going to have to stand accountable.

The Lord said: ". . .What hast thou done? the voice of thy brother's blood crieth unto me from the ground.

"And now art thou cursed from the earth, which hath opened her mouth to receive thy brother's blood from thy hand;

"When thou tillest the ground, it shall not henceforth yield unto thee her strength; a fugitive and a vagabond shalt thou be in the earth. . . .Therefore whosoever slayeth Cain, vengeance shall be taken on him sevenfold. And the Lord set a mark upon Cain, lest any finding him should kill him" (Gen. 4:10-12,15).

Notice what the Lord did not say: "Let's get rid of the knives so this won't happen again." Today we would say, "Let's look into knife legislation."

I read in a newspaper that a man was stabbed to death with a screwdriver and another man was beaten to death with a hammer. Are we going to pass legislation to get rid of guns, then hammers, next screwdrivers?

Knives don't kill people any more than hammers, screwdrivers, cars, or guns kill people. People kill people.

A person has a right to own a gun in this country. And I feel that when somebody buys a gun there should be a six-week mandatory training period to teach him how to use and respect the gun. We train a person more thoroughly in learning how to drive a car than we do in learning how to use a gun.

With Cain's punishment, the Lord set a precedent that criminals must be separated from society. At that time, He had not established capital punishment — the taking of someone's life as punishment for a severe crime. (See the discussion later in this book.) Where there was no law, God could not implement a law after the fact, then go back and make the person guilty for something for which there was no law. Because God had not established capital punishment, Cain could not be slain as a punishment. So instead, in essence, God imprisoned Cain. Because there were no prisons on earth, God imprisoned Cain with a curse: nothing would grow by his hands and wherever he went he would be an outcast. God put a mark on Cain to separate him from society. Without the bars, this was the first jail sentence.

The Lord also established that vigilantism — the action a group of people take to carry out a punishment based on their own decision — is wrong. When Cain said, ". . .it shall come to pass, that every one that findeth me shall slay me" (Gen. 4:14), the Lord said, ". . .whosoever slayeth Cain, vengeance shall be taken on him sevenfold. And the Lord set a mark upon Cain, lest any finding him should kill him" (Gen. 4:15). This verse, I believe, reveals to us the reason that God established capital punishment. Without a punishment equal to the crime, vigilante groups would be out everywhere, seeking the blood of those who had harmed them.

You may have had a loved one who was slain or murdered. He may have been killed because somebody was drunk — at fault — and the law let the other person go free without punishment. The thought may have crossed your mind to take vengeance into your own hands.

We can see from Genesis 4:15 that God does not want us to take vengeance into our own hands. By doing that, we are actually stepping over into God's territory. Romans 12:19 says: ". . .Vengeance is mine; I will repay, saith the Lord." And God can do a much better job than we can.

The blood of innocent slain people is still crying to the Lord from the ground. Isaiah 26:21 is referring to the Second Coming of the Lord: "For, behold, the Lord cometh out of his place to punish the inhabitants of the earth for their iniquity: the earth also shall disclose her blood, and shall no more cover her slain." There will come a day when the earth will open up and all that blood will be revealed. In the meantime, the best thing you can do for yourself instead of taking vengeance is to roll that problem over on the Lord. If you ever did try to take vengeance into your own hands, you would just bring more problems on yourself than you have now.

Capital Punishment —

The Bible shows us in both the Old and New Testaments that God condones capital punishment. This form of punishment was introduced into the world after the Flood when God said to Noah and his sons: "Whoso sheddeth man's blood, by man shall his blood be shed: for in the image of God made he man." (Gen. 9:6).

Romans 13:4 refers to capital punishment: "For he (meaning the government leader) is the minister of God to thee for good. But if thou do that which is evil, be afraid; for he beareth not the sword in vain: for he is the minister of God, a revenger to execute wrath upon him that doeth evil." The "sword" in this verse refers to capital punishment. The ruler does not bear the sword for no reason, but as a revenger upon the person who does evil.

Someone may say, "Yes, but what about Exodus 20:13, the Sixth Commandment, which says, 'Thou shalt not kill'?"

If the Bible says, "Thou shalt not kill" and also condones capital punishment, God contradicts Himself, and we know that God cannot contradict Himself. (Num. 23:19.)

The God Who said, "Thou shalt not kill," also commanded the children of Israel to go into Canaan and kill all the adults, all the children, and all the animals. (Deut. 20:16,17; Josh. 6:21; 10:40.)

When Moses came down from Mount Sinai where he had been forty days receiving the moral commandments of God, the Ten Commandments, and other "divers laws and ordinances," he found the Israelites worshipping idols. (Ex. 20-32.) Moses gave the people opportunities to repent. When he said, "Who is on the Lord's side? let him come unto me. . ." (Ex. 32:26) and the sons of Levi came, but three thousand did not, the same God Who a few days before gave Moses for the children of Israel the commandment "Thou shalt not kill," told Moses to ". . .Put every man his sword by his side, and go in and out from gate to gate throughout the camp, and slay every man his brother, and every man his companion, and every man his neighbour" (v. 27).

These incidents appear to be a contradiction, but once we examine them closely we find out they are not.

In Exodus 20:13 the word *kill* is from the Hebrew word *ratsach* which means to commit murder. The commandment does not mean "thou shalt not kill," but it means, "thou shalt not murder." Ecclesiastes 3:3 tells us there is "A time to kill, and a time to heal. . ." There is never a time for murder.

Proverbs 6:16 tells us, "These six things doth the Lord hate: yea, seven are an abomination unto him:. . ." The verse mentions only one outward sin and it is referring to murder: "hands that shed *innocent* blood." The Bible says that innocent blood should not be spilled, but it does condone hands shedding *guilty* blood. Capital punishment, self-defense, and killing in defense of your country are all condoned in God's Word. Murder is the shedding of innocent blood, and this is what Exodus 20:13 is saying: "You shall not shed innocent blood."

The Sixth Commandment is mentioned in the New Testament in Matthew, chapter 19. The rich young ruler went to Jesus and said, "Good Master, what good thing shall I do, that I may have eternal life? And he" (Jesus) "said unto him, Why callest thou me good? there is none good but one, that is, God: but if thou wilt enter into life, keep the commandments" (vv. 16,17). When the young ruler asked, "Which?" Jesus began with the Sixth Commandment from Exodus 20:13: "Thou shalt do no murder..." (v. 18). In the entire *King James Version* this verse is the *only* instance in which that commandment is translated correctly: "do no murder" instead of "not kill." God condones killing, but never murder. Murder, homicide, is always wrong. "Whoso sheddeth man's blood..." refers here to murder; "...by man shall his blood be shed..." refers to capital punishment. (Gen. 9:6.)

Someone may say, "What about Jesus' statement to Peter after Peter pulled out his sword and cut off the ear of the man who came to arrest Jesus? Jesus healed the ear and said, '...Put up again thy sword into his place: for all they that take the sword shall perish with the sword.' Wasn't he saying that it's not right for us to kill people, because we'll be killed ourselves?" (John 18:10; Luke 22:51; Matt. 26:52.)

Jesus was referring to criminals when He said "they that take the sword" and referring to capital punishment when He said "shall perish with the sword." Jesus was saying, "Peter you just cut off the ear of an official who represents the minister of God, and even though he's not doing right in arresting Me, you have no right to take vengeance into your hand against him. Roll off the problem on the Father, because capital punishment is right. If you kill the official, your life may be taken as punishment."

Satan has declared all-out war on the Kingdom of God to try to stop the gospel of the Lord Jesus Christ from reaching the lost. Crime is a part of Satan's attack.

When crime, anarchy and rebellion are on the rise in a country, preaching God's Word becomes more and more difficult. God wants crime stopped so much that he even condones capital punishment to take murderers out of the way so that the righteous can flourish. Proverbs 28:28 says:

"When the wicked rise, men hide themselves: but when they perish, the righteous increase." When wicked men perish instead of increasing, then the righteous can increase.

Remember, however, that murderers on death row are sinners who need to know Jesus. I believe death row is a good place to get people born again. After all, those people are thinking of what will happen to them when they die. We need to minister salvation to them. And after they receive the Lord, we can pray for God's mercy to be bestowed on them and that they could be pardoned and released. But if they are not released, they have a home in heaven.

5

Stopping Immorality

As we study the nation of Israel as our example of how a nation can prosper if it follows after God's Word, let's look at the second category of the symptoms of disease in a nation that Hosea 4:2 deals with: immorality, specifically *committing adultery*.

When God is not number one, when people begin to put their own rights, their own feelings of the flesh above everything else, standards change, and immorality rises. Today the moral standards have dropped to the point that talk of adultery has become part of the daily routine — on television adultery is glorified, something to laugh at. It is common for someone in a program to have two or three affairs at once. We can see from this type of generally accepted entertainment just how far the morals of the country have dropped.

The Bible has something to say about immorality. In Leviticus chapter 18, the Lord instructs Moses in His statutes for the children of Israel regarding acts of immorality. He describes the things in which they are not to defile themselves: incest (vv. 6-16), adultery (v. 20), homosexuality (v. 22), and bestiality (v. 23).

Verses 24 and 25 state: "Defile not ye yourselves in any of these things: for in all these the nations are defiled which I cast out before you: And the land is defiled: therefore I do visit the iniquity thereof upon it, and the land itself vomiteth out her inhabitants." This chapter refers to these acts of immorality as abominations.

Today some people call homosexuality an alternative lifestyle. Some even try to make homosexuality something spiritual, forming homosexual churches. Homosexuality is an abomination, an abhorrence, a perversion before God — we can see from the passage above and from the New Testament (Rom. 1:26,27) that He hates it. But God's power is available to deliver homosexuals and set them free. God hates homosexuality, but loves the homosexual and wants him set free.

In verse 2 *break out* means to leave or violate the boundaries. When a nation's people begin to leave the boundaries of God's Word, crime breaks out and morals decline because anything becomes excusable. The people of that nation think that in the name of freedom, they have a right to do whatever they want, never caring if they violate the freedoms of others. When freedom becomes license, anarchy is next. People "break out" of their boundaries.

When people are ignorant of God's Word, His standards and His morals, they find they can easily violate any law. Boundaries must be kept from one generation to another or moral decay sets in. Only the standards of God's Word give the power to keep the guidelines safe in our lifetime and in our children's lifetime. Parents cannot expect children to remain in line simply because "that's the way things are." But with God's authority enforcing the boundary, one generation can teach another about the importance of God's Word — that it is still true, that there are consequences of sin (violating His standards), and that there are blessings for abiding in His Word.

Today society challenges people to go ahead and find out what the other side is like. People do not understand that on the other side of moral law stands God. Law did not originate with man; it originated with God. Therefore, enforcement also originated with God. All men will stand before Him whether sinner or saint and give an account.

The problems we have today are not new. We are seeing from studying Hosea, chapter 4, that Israel had the same kinds of problems. We may have different names for them: pornography, homosexuality, sexual permissiveness, and abortion, but there is nothing new under the sun. We have a high divorce rate today because we have left the standard of God's Word. People do not see marriage as a covenant. A covenant demands commitment from both sides.

In America the military has weakened drastically, illegal drug use has increased, the quality of education has dropped. In our schools there are fewer regulations, less discipline, less learning.

Verse 2 says, "blood toucheth blood." Violence breeds more violence, murder breeds more murder, lying breeds more lying, adultery breeds more adultery. These types of incidents just breed more like them. There is a pattern to it: as violence begins, it continues to increase if there are no boundaries to stop it. People then wonder, "Where will it all end?"

Verse 3 begins: "Therefore shall the land mourn,..." The whole nation was in mourning because the people were in confusion — they did not understand why all those terrible things were happening. Today the nation mourns, and the majority of people are in confusion. They listen to the news and to their neighbors' reports of crime, and they wonder, "Why is this happening?" Yet God's Word tells us why it is happening: because the Truth, God's Word, has been taken out of the land.

Verse 3 continues: "...and every one that dwelleth therein shall languish,..." In this verse *languish* means to mourn in sadness. The inhabitants are in pain because without God's Word there are only problems. Today the world is screaming with problems, but has no answers. The world calls this the new age, the new morality. There is nothing new — it is the same devil with the same problems.

". . .with the beasts of the field, and with the fowls of heaven; yea, the fishes of the sea also shall be taken away." Why are animals becoming extinct? Why is the environment being so shaken? Why do we have pollution, acid rains? Environment cannot be legislated: when God's Words are taken out of the land and man suffers and is in confusion, even nature suffers. But when God's Words are in a nation, even the animals are blessed.

Verse 4 begins: "Yet let no man strive, nor reprove another: for thy people are as they that strive with the priest." The world blames other people for its problems: Democrats blame Republicans and Republicans blame Democrats. Incumbent legislators blame their predecessors. Verse 4 is saying that we should not point the finger of blame at other people. The cause of blame is really us for leaving God's Word. When a nation goes under, it is the fault of the Church. If an ineffective leader is in office, if legislation is bad, a nation can still survive if the salt of the earth refuses to lose its savour.

We left the principles of God's Word when we listened to the world which says, "Don't accept anything," and challenged God's authority and the authority of the ministers preaching the Word. We challenged God's authority when we read or heard the Word preached and said, "Prove it. I don't believe it." There is nothing wrong with our questioning God about His Word to gain a deeper understanding, but a nation which blatantly violates and challenges the authority of God's Word and those who preach it is headed for destruction.

When people leave God's Word, they begin to rebel against authority. A common saying in the late fifties and early sixties was, "God is dead," and during the sixties we saw a lot of rebellion against authority: people rebelled against the military by burning their draft cards, against the police department, against the nation itself. By the seventies, a general permissiveness had crept in. But today the "silent majority" is no longer silent — people who know God's Word are standing up and declaring, not their opinions, but what is right.

Verse 5 states: "Therefore shalt thou fall in the day, and the prophet also shall fall with thee in the night, and I will destroy thy mother." Those people who have challenged the priests shall stumble in the day and the prophet (false prophets) will fall with them in the night (the day of judgment).

The false prophets of Hosea's day had told the people not to listen to God's prophets. They told them that there was not any judgment coming and that the surrounding nations were not really evil, but peaceful. These statements sound a lot like ones we hear some liberal politicians and theologians make. The mother, false religion, had turned the people away from the true God and allowed "doctrines of devils" to enter in. They challenged the authority of God's Word and challenged the prophets of God as to coming judgment.

Verse 6 says: "My people are destroyed for lack of knowledge: because thou hast rejected knowledge, I will also reject thee..." "My people" refers to God's people within a nation who are the salt of the earth, the preserver of the nation. Rejecting the authority of God's Word will destroy an entire nation.

Look again at verse 5 which states, "Therefore shalt thou fall in the day..." This means that nations can fall quickly. In one night, the whole nation of Babylon fell. Daniel, chapter 5, tells us that when Belshazzar, the last king of Babylon, used the priestly cups from the temple for his own party, a hand appeared and began to write on the wall. The words were interpreted to mean: "Thou art weighed in the balances, and art found wanting" (v. 27). Verses 30 and 31 tell us: "In that night was Belshazzar the king of the

Chaldeans slain. And Darius the Median took the kingdom..." Although what leads to destruction may take some time, destruction can happen very quickly. Remember, we are studying Israel in these verses as an example. When a nation falls internally, it is ripe to fall externally — a nation never falls externally unless it has fallen internally first.

All the problems discussed in verses 2 and 3 with the modern day names — pornography, abortion, homosexuality, and different crimes — as evil as they are, are symptoms of the worse evil, the disease itself: rejection of God's Word. We can become involved with the specific things that are wrong with a nation and try to correct them individually. But because each problem is only a symptom, once we correct it, it will return. We must eliminate the cause to heal the disease. We have a responsibility to vote, but the success of a nation does not depend upon its legislators; it depends upon the Church.

"Where will it all end?" It ends with us. We Christians can stop the works of the devil by rising up, preaching and ministering God's Word. Jesus Christ, the Son of God, the Word, is "the same yesterday, and today and for ever." It is the knowledge of God's Word that brings boundaries, morality, and peace into a country. For violating God's Word, the consequences are the same yesterday, today and forever, but for keeping God's Word the blessings are also the same yesterday, today, and forever. "Blessed is the nation whose God is the Lord" (Ps. 33:12).

There is an answer: Believers listening to God's Word in the land brings the nation back into God's blessings.

The Strength of a Nation —

We can see similarities between the Israel God was addressing as described in Hosea, chapter 4, and our nation today, but, praise God, there is a revival in the land. The

Church today is gaining back its savour and rising up to stop the influences of Satan.

The strength of a nation is in the people of God. The Lord said, "If *my* people, which are called by *my* name, shall humble themselves, and pray, and seek my face, and turn from their wicked ways; then will I hear from heaven, and will forgive their sin, and will heal their land" (2 Chron. 7:14).

To help our nation, the greatest thing we can do besides praying is to attend church and receive knowledge of God's Word. Then we should go into the world as the salt of the earth, spread the gospel, and become doers of the Word. It is here that we gain God's strength: the knowledge of God will preserve the land.

6

Is World Peace Possible?

In the last few chapters we studied the principles that lead to the prosperity or decline of a nation based on the example of Israel from Hosea, chapter 4. In the next few chapters, we will examine in detail the principles God's Word teaches about militarily protecting a nation so that it can have peace and prosperity — an environment to more easily spread the gospel.

In Matthew, chapter 24, we read of the end times. (According to Bible prophecy, we are living in those times now!) Until Jesus Himself comes back to this earth, we will hear of "wars" (hot wars) "and rumours of wars" (cold wars) (v. 6). Jesus tells us not to be deceived.

". . .the disciples came unto him privately, saying, Tell us, when shall these things be? and what shall be the sign of thy coming, and of the end of the world? And Jesus answered and said unto them, Take heed that no man deceive you.

"For many shall come in my name, saying, I am Christ; and shall deceive many" (vv. 3-5). Still talking about not being deceived, Jesus continues: "And ye shall hear of wars and rumours of wars: see that ye be not troubled: for all these things must come to pass, but the end is not yet.

"For nation shall rise against nation, and kingdom against kingdom: and there shall be famines, and pestilences, and earthquakes, in divers places.

"All these are the beginning of sorrows" (vv. 6-8).

Today some people are trying to deceive us, saying that we can do away with war and usher in peace in our lifetime. Many of these people are sincere, but sincerely wrong, deceived. They are misled by false teachings, scriptures from God's Word pulled out of context. Do not let them deceive you. Even though in these end times you will hear of wars and rumors of wars, remember that Jesus said not to be troubled. We Christians do not need to fear!

I do not intend to demean the organizations trying to bring world peace — they have helped bring some peace, but that peace is always temporary. They are deceived because they cannot bring complete peace, lasting peace. Let's examine a passage of scripture which describes the time that Jesus will set up His Millennial Kingdom on this earth after His return and the Battle of Armageddon. (Satan is the author of war, so as long as Satan is on earth, there will be wars. Once Satan is cast out of this earth, at the time that Jesus comes to take his throne, all war will stop — Rev. 20:1-3.)

Isaiah 2:2-4 states:

And it shall come to pass in the last days, that the mountain of the Lord's house shall be established in the top of the mountains, and shall be exalted above the hills; and all nations shall flow unto it.

And many people shall go and say, Come ye, and let us go up to the mountain of the Lord, to the house of the God of Jacob; and he will teach us of his ways, and we will walk in his paths: for out of Zion shall go forth the law, and the word of the Lord from Jerusalem.

And he shall judge among the nations, and shall rebuke many people: and they shall beat their swords into plowshares, and their spears into pruninghooks: nation shall not lift up sword against nation, neither shall they learn war any more.

Organizations which refer to the portion of verse 4 which says "...they shall beat their swords into plowshares, and their spears into pruninghooks..." are quoting it out of context and changing its meaning. In context we see that the peace described in verse 4 will occur on the day that Jesus (not man) causes it to happen: the day that He returns to this earth. Until that day, we had better not beat our war weapons into peaceful tools, because we will need to defend our nation.

First Thessalonians 5:3 states: "For when they shall say, Peace and safety; then sudden destruction cometh upon them...and they shall not escape." Man's peace cannot last. Only the Lord Jesus Christ, the Prince of Peace (Is. 9:6), can bring permanent peace to the earth.

National Defense —

Destruction comes to a nation usually through military defeat. Military preparedness keeps a nation from being attacked and enables it to defend itself to protect its people.

Jesus said, "...how can one enter into a strong man's house, and spoil his goods, except he first bind the strong man? and then he will spoil his house" (Matt. 12:29). Jesus was saying that when you go into a strong man's house, you had better make sure you are stronger than he is. A nation which is well-defended stops other nations from attacking it. We discussed that America's freedom has been purchased by war. We see throughout God's Word that the way Israel stayed in peace was by winning war. Israel did not go into war halfway; Israel went in to win. Today the term "non-aggressive" war is used. Has anyone ever heard of a non-aggressive football team? A football team goes in there to win. That is what a nation should do in war.

Throughout the Bible we see examples of nations kept free because of military victory. We can see one of these examples in Nehemiah, chapter 4. After the captivity of

Babylon, Nehemiah led a group of Israelites, who had been in captivity for seventy years, back to Jerusalem to rebuild the city, the wall, and the temple. Most of the group had been born in captivity, and even though they were young people, were physically weak.

The nations around Jerusalem were angry, thinking the Israelites planned to build another empire and destroy the surrounding nations. Four nations began to mass together to attack the few weak Israelites. In the natural realm the Israelites were out numbered. But, as Elisha's servant saw after Elisha prayed that his servant's eyes be opened to see that the mountain was full of horses and chariots on their side, there were more with Nehemiah than there were with them, the enemy. (2 Kings 6:16.)

Nehemiah, who is narrating, states: "And conspired all of them together to come and to fight against Jerusalem, and to hinder it. Nevertheless we made our prayer unto our God, and set a watch against them day and night, because of them" (Neh. 4:8,9).

The adversaries told the Jews ten times that they were going to attack the Jews from all directions. (v. 12.) Fear probably went through the people's hearts. They probably thought, "We're mainly families; we aren't all warriors. What are we going to do?" They did the only thing they knew to do: they prayed.

Nehemiah set around the city what few people there were to defend it and protect themselves. He said, ". . . Be not ye afraid of them: remember the Lord, which is great and terrible, and fight for your brethren, your sons, and your daughters, your wives, and your houses" (v. 14).

Verse 15 states, "And it came to pass, when our enemies heard that it was known unto us, and God had brought their counsel to nought, that we returned all of us to the wall, every one unto his work." The four nations were planning to attack as long as the Israelites were defenseless, but when the few rose up and prepared for battle, the other nations backed away!

Verse 16 shows us that Nehemiah learned a lesson: "And it came to pass from that time forth, that the half of my servants wrought in the work, and the other half of them held both the spears, the shields, and the bows, and the habergeons;" (*breastplates*) "and the rulers" (*captains*) "were behind all the house of Judah." Nehemiah cut the work force in half: half built the wall, half formed the military. He learned that a nation prepared for defense is a deterrent to war. Adversaries will think twice before attacking a well-armed nation.

America is not a nation that forces war or makes the first move to attack nations just to be aggressive. Nehemiah 4:14 tells us that God calls a nation to protect its brothers, sisters, wives, children — its families, its households. What God has freely given us Satan would love to take from us by destroying it. When our peace, the safety of our families, is threatened and another nation aggressively comes against us, we should go in there and win! We should back that nation off and say, "Don't do it again." Military strength impresses nations. Today people should find out God's will, fight for their country and be patriots for the Lord.

Francis Scott Key, the author of "The Star-Spangled Banner," America's national anthem, knew that it was war that made this nation free. He was inspired to write the poem during a time of war about war. When the battle was over and he looked up and saw the flag still there, the scene represented to him that America was going to make it.

The third verse describes where we are today:

Oh, thus be it ever when freemen shall
    stand

Between their lov'd home and the war's
   desolation!

Blest with vict'ry and peace
   may the heav'n-rescued land

Praise the power that hath made
   and preserv'd us a nation!

Then conquer we must,
   when our cause it is just,

And this be our motto, 'In God is our
   Trust,'

And the star-spangled banner in triumph
   shall wave

O'er the land of the free and the home
   of the brave.

7
Fighting To Defend the Nation

In the Bible God condones killing under two different circumstances. We have already discussed the first: capital punishment. The second, fighting for our country — and killing — to defend it is not only condoned in God's Word; it is commanded. And we can do it in the name of the Lord knowing we are preserving freedom. The sword of capital punishment and the sword of war is not the same as the sword of murder.

Hebrews, chapter 11, which describes the great heroes of faith, tells us of people who went to war in the Old Testament. The chapter lists the heroes and describes briefly what each did by faith. Verses 32 and 33 state: "And what shall I more say? for the time would fail me to tell of Gedeon, and of Barak, and of Samson, and of Jephthae: of David also, and Samuel, and of the prophets: Who through faith subdued kingdoms..."

Gedeon, Barak, Jephthae and David were men of war. What they did by faith was succeed in war. Nothing else is told us about Barak, and Jephthae and Gedeon except that they were mighty men during battle and that God was with them in war.

David was a man for peace. But when aggressive nations warred against him, he became a man of war and called upon the strength of the Lord to help him. David said, "In my distress I cried unto the Lord, and he heard me... Woe is me, that I sojourn in Mesech, that I dwell in the tents of

Kedar! My soul hath long dwelt with him that hateth peace. I am for peace: but when I speak, they are for war" (Ps. 120:1,5-7). (David is using the names "Mesech" and "Kedar" to mean those who are the enemy; he may not actually have been physically in those places.)

The word *subdue* means to put under foot. In Hebrews 11:33 it means to annihilate and destroy. The same faith that heals, that saves, that meets needs; the same faith that caused Enoch to walk with God (Gen. 5:24; Heb. 11:5), Noah to build an ark (Heb. 11:7), and Abraham to become the father of our faith (Gal.3:8) is the same faith that will be with men in battle to subdue kingdoms. God will be with us to preserve us and help us defeat the enemy in battle. And we can do it all in the name of the Lord.

Some of the greatest patriots in America's history went to war trusting in the Lord and experienced His preservation. They subdued kingdoms and fought against enemies of our nation. We are free today because of men who fought for this country and knew how to trust God in the midst of war: men like George Washington at Valley Forge, and Benjamin Franklin who in a call for prayer, called on ". . .the Father of Lights to illuminate our understanding."

". . .wrought righteousness, obtained promises, stopped the mouths of lions, Quenched the violence of fire, *escaped the edge of the sword*. . ." (vv. 33,34). All of this is still "through faith" (which begins v. 33). In battle, by faith, they were preserved from being killed.

Psalm 91:7 states: "A thousand shall fall at thy side, and ten thousand at thy right hand; but it shall not come nigh thee." I've heard of soldiers who put that verse in their helmets. When they take their helmet off at night, they are reminded of God's keeping power. We can go to war in faith.

Verse 34 continues: ". . .escaped the edge of the sword, *out of weakness were made strong, waxed valiant in fight, turned to flight the armies of the aliens.*"

God's Word (still referring to war) can change weak people into courageous people. They can become so strong, so valiant in fight, that they turn to flight the armies of foreigners (the aliens). The armies of the enemy who were not destroyed, turned and ran! Throughout the Bible we read accounts of enemy forces who became disoriented, fearful and killed themselves. The survivors fled from God's people. (Josh. 10:10,11; Judges 7:19-22; 1 Sam. 30:16,17.)

Peace Is Purchased through War —

A number of people have called themselves conscientious objectors on the basis of the one verse of scripture: "Thou shalt not kill." They say that going to war and killing people is murder. They say they will not go to war and fight because it is their freedom. Freedom is purchased through blood. Our parents and grandparents went to war and shed blood — many of them came back wounded — so that people could have the freedom to say, "I won't fight."

Ecclesiastes 3:1,3,8 says that there is ". . .a time to every purpose under the heaven. . ." that there is, "A time to kill, and a time to heal; . . .a time of war, and a time of peace. . ."

This nation was fought for; people bled and died on battlefields to purchase the freedom of this country. Peace is purchased through war. Why are we at peace in America today? Because somebody paid for it, somebody fought for it, somebody went to war and purchased our freedom.

David was a man of war, but Solomon had peace built on the wars of his father David. His father purchased the peace for a generation to come. We have the right to bear arms, to go to war, and to preserve and fight for our country according to the Constitution of the United States. We have a right to stand up for our country, to wear its uniform proudly, to go into battle and kill the enemy in the name of the Lord. We have a right to rejoice in that we are preserving freedom, including the right to worship God in a nation that honors and respects that right.

If America were attacked by another nation wanting to enslave us, we have the God-given right to stand up and say, "I'll fight to keep my freedom." And we can go to war and believe God will be with us in war and in battle. Conscientious objectors and other able-bodied people who refuse to fight for other reasons (disobedience, as in the case of the tribes of Reuben and Gad, and fear, as in the case of those two tribes' fathers) discourage the others who are fighting.

In Numbers, chapter 32, we read of a group of Israelites who told Moses that they did not want to fight. The tribes of Reuben and Gad wanted to settle in the land of Jazer and Gilead, where they felt comfortable, rather than going with the other Israelites to fight for the land of Canaan, for the country, that God had promised them.

Moses answered: ". . . Shall your brethren go to war, and shall ye sit here? And wherefore discourage ye the heart of the children of Israel from going over into the land which the Lord hath given them?" (vv. 6,7).

Moses also said: "And, behold, ye are risen up in your fathers' stead, an increase of sinful men, to augment yet the fierce anger of the Lord toward Israel" (v. 14).

Numbers, chapters 13 and 14, gives us the account of the twelve men of Israel, the "fathers" of Numbers 32:14, sent to spy out the promised land. Two, Joshua and Caleb, came back with a good report, because they compared the giants they saw there to God's promise. They remembered He had already given them the land. Their standard was God's Word. They knew that with the power of God they could overcome the giants.

The men of Numbers, chapter 32, who did not want to fight were committing the sins of their fathers, ten of whom, after spying out the promised land, came back with an evil report. They said they were as grasshoppers by comparison to the giants they had seen. They "discouraged the heart of the children of Israel, that they should not go into the land which the Lord had given them." (v. 9).

In the end, all twelve tribes of Israel fought to possess the land and, with God working powerfully for them, conquered the nation in five years. The closing verse of Joshua, chapter 11, says: "So Joshua took the whole land, according to all that the Lord said unto Moses; and Joshua gave it for an inheritance unto Israel according to their divisions by their tribes. And the land rested from war" (v. 23).

You should not settle for anything less than the promised land — what God has promised you — in your own life. No matter how big your giants are, they are grasshoppers in God's sight.

Turn the Other Cheek? —

Someone might ask why God instructed the Israelites to kill so many people when the Israelites took the promised land. Deuteronomy and Leviticus tell us that these nations were filled with sin so horrible that it could have infected the Israelites.

Someone might ask, "But doesn't the Bible tell us to 'Turn the other cheek'?"

Jesus said: "Ye have heard that it hath been said, An eye for an eye, and a tooth for a tooth:

"But I say unto you, That ye resist not evil: but whosoever shall smite thee on thy right cheek, turn to him the other also.

"And if any man will sue thee at the law, and take away thy coat let him have thy cloak also.

"And whosoever shall compel thee to go a mile, go with him twain.

"Give to him that asketh thee, and from him that would borrow of thee turn thou not away.

"Ye have heard that it hath been said, Thou shalt love thy neighbour, and hate thine enemy.

"But I say unto you, Love your enemies, bless them that curse you, do good to them that hate you, and pray for them which despitefully use you, and persecute you" (Matt. 5:38-44).

Jesus makes two statements that at first reading almost seem to contradict each other. Let's look carefully at what Jesus was saying. The first part of verse 38 is a quote from the Old Testament: "Eye for eye, tooth for tooth." (Ex. 21:24; Lev. 24:20; Deut. 19:21.)

The contexts of the quotes in the Old Testament reveal that Jesus was referring to the way a judge handles a case in court. In other words, the punishment is to fit the crime. The Jews' bringing this verse into the New Testament times has perverted its meaning by making it appear that Jesus is breaking the law by preaching mercy. In verse 39 Jesus is bringing out the exception to the rule: ". . . but whosoever shall smite thee on thy right cheek, turn to him the other also."

After reading those verses we may think, "An eye for an eye and a tooth for a tooth is Old Testament. The New Testament teaches to love everybody — your enemies, those who despitefully use you — because now that we're in the New Testament times we have a different law than in the Old Testament."

God does not change. Adultery and telling lies in the Old Testament is just as wrong as adultery and telling lies in the New Testament. Today our court systems still need to operate according to God's Word as much as they did in Old Testament times. Jesus was bringing out that the issue was being confused. The principle which should have been applied to court cases was being applied to everyday life, in relationships with one another.

Jesus laid the background for these statements when in the Sermon on the Mount, He said: "Blessed are the peacemakers: for they shall be called the children of God.

"Blessed are they which are persecuted for righteousness' sake: for theirs is the kingdom of heaven.

"Blessed are ye, when men shall revile you, and persecute you, and shall say all manner of evil against you falsely, for my sake.

"Rejoice, and be exceeding glad: for great is your reward in heaven. . ." (Matt. 5:9-12).

According to this verse, a peacemaker is a witness for Jesus Christ — someone who is called a child of God. Notice that witnessing does not make someone a child of God; it lets it be known that he is a child of God. Someone makes it known he is a child of God by opening his mouth and telling people about the Lord Jesus.

Mark 16:15 tells us to "Go ye into all the world, and preach the gospel to every creature." This is not just for missionaries, but for every believer. In this book we are discussing the special importance of spreading the gospel so that more believers are able to unite in prayer for the nation.

Matthew 5:10 should not be quoted out of context, because the "they" of verse 10 who are persecuted are "the peacemakers" of verse 9 who are witnessing for the Lord. In verse 39, Jesus is saying that when you are persecuted because of your witness, when men revile you, and say all manner of evil against you falsely *for Jesus' sake,* then do not retaliate: turn the other cheek.

In verse 39 Jesus is talking about witnessing for Him, not referring in any way to defending our country. He does not mean that when armies attack our country, we are to turn the other cheek, love them, put our arms around them and hug them. He is saying that when we are persecuted for witnessing for the Lord Jesus Christ, we are to turn the other cheek.

I heard the testimony of the leader of a motorcycle gang who, before he was born again, was the toughest one of the gang. He said it took a long time for that meanness to get out of him. He forced the other bikers to receive Jesus by pounding them in the face or physically forcing them in some other way. That's not the way we witness for the Lord according to what Jesus is saying in verse 39.

We do not win people to the Lord with fists — we do not beat the gospel into them. When we witness and people persecute and slap us for it, we are to turn the other cheek. Seeing Jesus and the manifestation of His love in us causes people to come to the Lord, not violence. ". . .the goodness of God leadeth thee to repentance. . ." (Rom. 2:4).

8

God Ordained the Military

God has ordained the military to preserve and keep a nation. He has promised that if the military will look for direction from Him, He will give it supernatural power to fight against the enemy.

Numbers, chapter 1, tells us how God ordained the military to be set up in the days of Israel. The children of Israel had recently come out into the wilderness and were unorganized. God instructed Moses:

"Take ye the sum of all the congregation of the children of Israel, after their families, by the house of their fathers, with the number of their names, every male by their polls; from twenty years old and upward, all that are able to go forth to war in Israel: thou and Aaron shall number them by their armies" (vv. 2,3).

God's instructions were to form an army from *all* the males who were able to fight. This army was not voluntary — the people in it were drafted. (Incidentally, notice that males were not to join until they reached the age of twenty years old — men, not boys.)

Deuteronomy, chapter 24, gives us the one exception to being drafted: being a newlywed!

"When a man hath taken a new wife, he shall not go out to war, neither shall he be charged with any business: but he shall be free at home one year, and shall cheer up his wife which he hath taken" (v. 5).

After marrying, a man was given exemption from fighting for one year to "cheer up his wife," in other words, to love her for one year. After a year, he had something worth fighting for. He was fighting not only to protect the nation, but to protect what he had personally in his home. Remember we learned from Nehemiah 4:14 that we are fighting to protect our families, our homes.

Instruct Your Children —

We must instruct our children in patriotism and in the importance of fighting for our country. We must instill in our children the promises of God. Deuteronomy 6:6,7 tells us: "And these words, which I command thee this day, shall be in thine heart: And thou shalt teach them diligently unto thy children, and shalt talk of them when thou sittest in thine house, and when thou walkest by the way, and when thou liest down, and when thou risest up."

Our children must know that the military is ordained of God, and as members of the military, they can go into battle in confidence that they will not go under. They will be protected by God's Word instilled in them. In the worst of circumstances and unfair situations, they will have one person to preserve them in the midst of battle who is always fair: Jesus. Fear may try to come, but they will know God's love, and "perfect love casteth out fear" (1 John 4:18). In the military they can minister to others around them to help bring those people through victoriously.

Judges, chapter 3, shows us that each generation was taught by its parents to fight for the nation. "Now these are the nations which the Lord left, to prove Israel by them, even as many of Israel as had not known all the wars of Canaan; Only that the generations of the children of Israel might know, to teach them war, at the least such as before knew nothing thereof." (vv. 1,2).

It was not God's will for an entire generation of the enemy to be killed. He wanted some of them "left" so that the children of Israel could be instructed in the ways of war.

We can see that God ordained the military. David said, "Blessed be the Lord my strength, which teacheth my hands to war, and my fingers to fight" (Ps. 144:1). Patriotism, the desire to fight for your country, that rises up inside you is from God.

The Bible tells of the days when the armies came home and the people gave glory to God because they won the war. First Samuel 18:6 and 7 tells us that when David came home from battle, the women sang and danced with joy, and said, "Saul hath slain his thousands, and David his ten thousands," giving glory to the Lord for the preservation of the nation. Thank God for the people who fought to preserve freedom in the earth in the world wars, in Korea, and in Vietnam.

Once after I had been teaching for a few weeks on the subject of war and supporting the military, a number of Vietnam veterans came up to talk to me afterward. They said that I was the first person they had ever heard openly declare that he was proud of what they had done in Vietnam. Shortly after that, I received a letter from a lieutenant colonel who had been in active duty in the Army during the Vietnam War.

He wrote:

. . .You were correct when you stated that the morale of the troops becomes low when people do not support the military. I had to counsel many during my three years, as it was very hard to keep a positive attitude, when those at home were so negative. . .

If we have to go to war again (and I hope we never do), we, the salt of the earth, who will not be trodden under the foot of men, will rise up and fight as the Word says to fight.

The Leader of God's Army —

Jesus is the Lord of Hosts. One translation calls Him Jehovah of Armies. Jesus is the commander of God's host, the armies of heaven; the highest ranking officer in all of God's army; and He has set the precedent in fighting wars. Numbers 21:14 tells us of "the book of the wars of the Lord." God records the wars that He fights and wins in the book!

When we fight in the name of the Lord, we could each be fighting twenty men, and it would not matter because behind us is an army of innumerable members, that will fight with us — the Lord Jesus Christ and all the angels.

In Joshua, chapter 5, we read that Jesus appeared to Joshua ". . .as captain of the host of the Lord. . ." (v. 14). The Lord then gave Joshua council about the war.

Zechariah 14:3 is referring to the final Battle of Armageddon which Jesus will fight for Israel as He has fought other battles for Israel. "Then shall the Lord go forth, and fight against those nations, as when he fought in the day of battle."

Jesus holds the record for killing the most enemy in any battle. Isaiah 37:36 tells us: "Then the angel of the Lord went forth, and smote in the camp of the Assyrians a hundred and fourscore and five thousand" (185,000) "and when they arose early in the morning, behold, they were all dead corpses."

At the Battle of Armageddon Jesus will break his own record before He ushers in everlasting peace.

Revelation 19:11 says:

And I saw heaven opened, and behold a white horse; and he that sat upon him was called Faithful and True, and in righteousness he doth judge and make war.

(Notice that in righteousness we can fight wars.)

Verses 12 through 14:

His eyes were as a flame of fire, and on his head were many crowns; and he had a name written, that no man knew, but he himself.

And he was clothed with a vesture dipped in blood: and his name is called The Word of God. And the armies which were in heaven followed him upon white horses, clothed in fine linen, white and clean.

We believers and the angels that are returning with Jesus are in the armies of heaven. On that final day; however, none of the armies will fight. Jesus will fight this battle by Himself.

Revelation 19:15,16:

And out of his mouth goeth a sharp sword, that with it he should smite the nations: he shall rule them with a rod of iron: and he treadeth the winepress of the fierceness and wrath of Almighty God.

And he hath on his vesture and on his thigh a name written, King of Kings, and Lord of Lords.

Revelation 14:20:

And the winepress was trodden without the city, and the blood came out of the winepress, even unto the horse bridles, by the space of a thousand and six hundred furlongs.

Romans 11:22 says, "Behold therefore the goodness and severity of God." God's goodness falls upon those who trust in Him and His severity upon those who reject Him. On the final day, Jesus returns — one Man destroys all the armies of the world.

With the Battle of Armageddon, Jesus will finally end all war. But until that day, God's power and His army are behind us when we go to war in the name of the Lord.

Waging War in Righteousness —

In Revelation 19:11 we saw that when Jesus returns, He will make war in righteousness. In righteous war we are fighting for godly principles with God Himself backing us in the fight.

Skill in war comes from God. First Chronicles 5:18 tells us that ". . .The sons of Reuben, and the Gadites, and half the tribe of Manasseh, of valiant men. . ." were ". . .skilful in war. . ." We also learn from this passage that when we cry out to God putting our trust in Him, He helps us. (v. 20.) The war was of God and many were slain. (v. 22.)

Organized armies are important. Jesus said, ". . .what king, going to make war against another king, sitteth not down first, and consulteth whether he be able with ten thousand to meet him that cometh against him with twenty thousand?" (Luke 14:31). When armies that are correctly trained lean on the arm of God in righteous war, God will back them with supernatural power. A few can slay many.

God delivers us in time of battle. David praised God for delivering him and making his way perfect when he was in difficult places: "God is my strength and power: and he maketh my way perfect. He maketh my feet like hinds' feet: and setteth me upon my high places" (2 Sam. 22:33,34). In the same passage, David said, "He teacheth my hands to war; so that a bow of steel is broken by mine arms" (v. 35). To break a steel bow with your natural strength is impossible, but with God's power in you, it is possible.

When Satan tries to steal our possessions or our health, we stand up with weapons (2 Cor. 10:4; Eph. 6:13-17) and fight him with the Word of God and the name of Jesus. But when an aggressive nation tries to take away our privileges and freedoms in this country, we question whether we should defend ourselves. This is Satan coming to steal from us on a national instead of a personal level. We have a right to stand up in the natural realm and fight for what God has given us.

9
Praying To Defend the Nation

Consult God —

Before a nation goes to war, its leaders should pray to consult God. "Every purpose is established by counsel:" (God's counsel, not man's) "and with good advice make war" (Prov. 20:18). Man is imperfect. Rather than depending on man's opinions, a nation's leaders should call in the prophets of the land to ask for God's wisdom and guidance.

"A wise man is strong; yea, a man of knowledge increaseth strength. For by wise counsel thou shalt make thy war: and in multitude of counsellors there is safety" (Prov. 24:5,6). The multitude of counsellors is composed of godly people who know the principles of God's Word. It is important to a nation's success in war that it understands the principles of God's Word and looks to the leadership and guidance of the ministries that God has placed within the land.

We see in the Bible that ministries were placed in Israel to instruct and guide kings. We have seen that the Church today is to subdue the land, to rise up and take dominion and authority. One way to accomplish this is to instruct the leadership of the land, to tell them what God has to say about war.

Proverbs 24:3,4 states: "Through wisdom is an house builded; and by understanding it is established: And by knowledge shall the chambers be filled with all precious and pleasant riches."

71

Our house, our nation, was built on the wisdom of God; it is still in existence because it was founded on the principles of God's Word. When our lives are established upon the Rock of the Lord Jesus Christ, the storms can come, the winds can come, but our house will not be touched.

Matthew 7:26 states: "And every one that heareth these sayings of mine, and doeth them not, shall be likened unto a foolish man, which built his house upon the sand: And the rain descended, and the floods came, and the winds blew, and beat upon that house; and it fell: and great was the fall of it."

There are people who study destruction, who study how to destroy other people. Proverbs 24:1 says: "Be not thou envious against evil men, neither desire to be with them. For their heart studieth destruction, and their lips talk of mischief."

Some nations delight in war, continually using their imaginations for war. Psalm 140:1,2 states: "Deliver me, O Lord, from the evil man: preserve me from the violent man; Which imagine mischiefs in their heart; continually are they gathered together for war."

David is referring to people who have no consideration for human life or for the freedom of others, but who choose to enslave and entrap people and steal from them. In David's day it was the Philistines, Assyrians, and Amalekites who were warlike; in World War II it was Hitler's Third Reich.

Today we must not be fooled by nations who say they want peace, but actually want war. We must be careful about entering into a covenant with them, because they may break it. Warlike nations may use a covenant to buy a little time of peace so that they may later destroy those with whom they have made peace.

A nation which establishes itself in war, in taking things from people, in destruction, does not have a solid foundation. An aggressive nation has built its house on sand, and something slight can cause it to crumble.

Touch Not God's Anointed —

The purpose of a country that honors God is to pray not only for goodness and prosperity to fill the land, but to pray against those nations antagonistic toward the country.

Psalm 68:30 shows us the attitude we are to take toward aggressive military nations. "Rebuke the company of spearmen, the multitude of the bulls," (*the aggressive nation's leaders*) "with the calves of the people," (*the military who follows the leaders*) "till every one submit himself with pieces of silver: scatter thou the people that delight in war."

This verse is telling intercessors to pray and rebuke these antagonistic leaders.

David prayed against his enemies who had decided to overthrow him. When David's son Absalom revolted against his father, he stole the hearts of all the people, even taking with him one of David's finest war counselors, Ahithophel, the one David could not stand to lose. Ahithophel knew David's thinking, his reactions, his deepest secrets and he could tell Absalom everything.

David prayed: "O Lord...turn the counsel of Ahithophel into foolishness" (2 Sam. 15:31). When Ahithophel counseled Absalom, he gave him the best counsel Absalom could have had. Ahithophel told Absalom exactly how to destroy David, yet God turned the counsel into foolishness. In the end Absalom followed foolish counsel instead of Ahithophel's counsel. When Ahithophel learned of this, he hanged himself.

We should pray for our enemies to come to know the Lord. We should pray for other nations to be evangelized. But First Chronicles 16:22 says, "Touch not mine anointed, and do my prophets no harm." A nation coming against us is touching God's anointed. When a nation has decided to pull out their weapons and destroy us, we have a right to get on our knees and pray, "God turn their plans into foolishness and cause them to come to naught. Disperse the enemy: scatter the people that delight in war."

Do Not Be Afraid —

When we see one nation after another falling to communism, when we realize we are outnumbered, we may want to ask, "What are we going to do?"

"Cast thy burden upon the Lord, and he shall sustain thee: he shall never suffer the righteous to be moved" (Ps. 55:22).

Remember that, as Elisha saw, there are more with us than there are with the enemy. Remember that we have the power of all God's army behind us when we trust in its leader, Jesus Christ. With an army of 300 men, Gideon defeated the huge army of the Midianites. (Judges 7.) We serve the Lord Jesus Christ Who in one night slew 185,000, and in the Battle of Armageddon will destroy all the armies of the world. And remember that Psalm 91:7 promises: "A thousand shall fall at thy side, and ten thousand at thy right hand; but it shall not come nigh thee."

If necessary, God will intervene in the natural realm to come to our defense. Psalm 46 was written after Jesus slew the 185,000. Verses 7 and 8 state: "The Lord of hosts is with us; the God of Jacob is our refuge. Selah. Come, behold the works of the Lord, what desolations he hath made in the earth."

Verse 9 tells us how the Lord makes "wars to cease unto the end of the earth; he breaketh the bow, and cutteth the spear in sunder; he burneth the chariot in the fire."

When you trust in the Lord, you can be surrounded by tanks in the middle of a field and not fear. God can break the machinery to bits.

In 1967 during the Six-Day War, when Israel's armies took back the city of Jerusalem, God moved to destroy the enemy. There were many testimonies of the enemy abandoning their tanks and equipment even though there were more of them than the Israelis. There were testimonies of angels that only the Israelis could see fighting for them. Many Israelis did not fight in their own strength, but in that of the Lord.

In Psalm 27:1-3 we can see the attitude God wants those in the military to have. "The Lord is my light and my salvation; whom shall I fear? the Lord is the strength of my life; of whom shall I be afraid?

"When the wicked, even mine enemies and my foes, came upon me to eat up my flesh, they stumbled and fell.

"Though an host should encamp against me, my heart shall not fear: though war should rise against me, in this will I be confident."

David was confident that the Lord was his light, his salvation, his refuge, and that he had no one to fear. When God becomes the strength of your life, you can go into the midst of battle, surrounded on all sides, and know the Lord will deliver you supernaturally.

"But thou, O God, shalt bring them" (the enemy) "down into the pit of destruction: bloody and deceitful men shall not live out half their days; but I will trust in thee" (Ps. 55:23).

Keep your faith and trust in the Lord. Psalm 91:16 says, "With long life will I satisfy him, and shew him my salvation."

We read in Deuteronomy 20:1 the advice Moses gives to those people going into battle for the first time: "When thou goest out to battle against thine enemies, and seest horses, and chariots, and a people more than thou, be not afraid of them: for the Lord thy God is with thee, which brought thee up out of the land of Egypt." He is saying even when it appears you are outnumbered by strong men of war who are better equipped than you, to not be afraid.

Probably one of the hardest things in the world to do when you are standing against incredible odds is to not be afraid. Verses 2-4: "And it shall be, when ye are come nigh unto the battle, that the priest shall approach and speak unto the people,

"And shall say unto them, Hear, O Israel, ye approach this day unto battle against your enemies: let not your hearts faint, fear not, and do not tremble, neither be ye terrified because of them;

"For the Lord your God is he that goeth with you, to fight for you against your enemies, to save you."

Can you see the importance of keeping your eyes on the Lord? When you go into battle, a priest may not be near to tell you what to do, but you can pull scriptures and promises God has given you out of your heart. And you can minister to those around you. In the battle, you can be a minister for the Lord.

Notice that the Lord goes out to smite the enemies, but He also goes out to save you. If Christ lives inside of you and He delivers you in war, don't you think He can deliver you in your home? In your finances? Don't you think He can deliver you from oppression or from bad circumstances in life? "If God be for us, who can be against us?" (Rom. 8:31).

If the Prince of Peace lives inside you, the whole world could fall apart, but you would not. The whole world could be short of food, but you would not be. ". . .yet have I not seen the righteous forsaken, nor his seed begging bread" (Ps. 37:25). You can be in the midst of war and have peace on the inside. No wonder we are more than conquerors through Jesus Who loved us. And in these times when we see symptoms of disease in our country, we can know that God can deliver us from all of them.

10
Separation of Church and State

In Matthew, chapter 22, Jesus gives us the proper attitude to have toward church and state. The Pharisees and the Herodians asked Jesus, "Is it lawful to give tribute unto Caesar, or not?" (v. 17).

Speaking of a penny, Jesus asked: "Whose is this image and superscription?" (v. 20).

They answered, ". . .Caesar's."

"Then saith he unto them, Render therefore unto Caesar the things which are Caesar's; and unto God the things that are God's" (v. 21).

Jesus was saying that we live in two worlds. We are to render to one world what belongs to it and to the other world what belongs to it. We are in the world, but not of it. Jesus said, "They" (the ones whom God has given Him) "are not of the world, even as I am not of the world" (John 17:16).

Even though church and state are on opposite sides of the coin, even though they are separate, they are joined together. Let's look at the example of marriage. You and your husband or wife are separate, but you are joined together. You are separate personalities who desire to flow together. One has to be in authority and one has to be in submission. (Eph. 5:22 says: "Wives, submit yourselves unto your own husbands, as unto the Lord.")

The same principle applies to church and state. Even though the government and the church are not the same, they need to line up and go in the same direction. "Can two walk together, except they be agreed?" (Amos 3:3). God has joined the two together, but one has to be an authority and one has to be in submission. God is the authority, and the proper way for government to flow with God is to be in submission to God.

We are to render certain things to the nation, to the state and the city we live in. But there are also things we are obligated to give to God. The things we are obligated to give man should never infringe upon the things we are obligated to give God.

Government is not church and church is not government. The government is not God. However, God does not want religion to control the state. When religion ran the state, the atrocity of the Spanish Inquisition occurred: millions of people were slaughtered in the name of religion. And when religion ran the state, Jesus was crucified on the cross.

Religion: the Enemy of Christianity —

In His day, Jesus faced the argument of whether church and state should be separated. However, it was religion, not so much government, that opposed Jesus.

The Pharisees and the Herodians hated each other. The Pharisees wanted control of the government, in the name of religion. The Herodians regarded Herod as their Lord and wanted him to set up his own empire. The Pharisees and the Herodians were both out to establish their own kingdoms, and Jesus was a threat to both of them.

Often people who hate each other will drop their differences to join against a common enemy. The Pharisees and Herodians, two die-hard enemies, joined together against their common enemy, Jesus. Once they destroyed Jesus, they would go back to fighting among themselves again. The Pharisees preached that salvation comes by works; by keeping the law; by circumcision; and naturally, by giving money. They desired power and money.

Jesus preached about redemption, that salvation comes by faith and not by works. Even though Jesus was not opposing the government, He became a threat because people by the thousands began to follow Him. He performed miracles and healed those who were sick in the multitudes. And to spread Himself further, He trained His disciples.

His enemies tried in every way to destroy Jesus. They tried to entangle Him, tried to show that He was against Moses, against the prophets. But every time they tried to entangle Him, they were the ones who ended up in their own trap.

The people in the established religion saw Jesus as a religious threat because multitudes were turning to follow Him and would eventually give Him their money. They also saw Him as a political threat. The people were hailing Jesus as a king.

The Pharisees met to try to find a way to get rid of Jesus. Matthew 22:15 says: "Then went the Pharisees, and took counsel how they might entangle him in his talk." The question quoted at the beginning of this chapter that the Pharisees and Herodians asked Jesus, "Is it lawful to give tribute unto Caesar, or not?" was an attempt to entrap Jesus.

First they tried to make him feel good by addressing him with a big title. They called Him "Master" even though they did not regard Him as Master. Then they tried to flatter Him further by telling Him that they knew He would speak the truth without caring what people thought. (Mark 12:14.) Even though that was true, they did not believe it. They were simply trying to fill Him with pride before delivering the blow by asking Him the loaded question.

The government of those times was not like our government. To them Caesar was lord. Today a question such as "Is it lawful to give tribute unto Caesar, or not?" would be like saying, "Is it lawful to give taxes to the government?" Of course, the answer today would be "yes." But if Jesus had answered "yes," He would have been saying that someone was higher than He was: Caesar. The group of people standing around Him would have thought, "Jesus speaks truth, we should go worship Caesar." This would have immediately taken away His spiritual kingdom.

If He had said "no," He would have been in violation politically. He could have been immediately taken to Rome for insurrection against the government and tried under Roman law.

The Pharisees and Herodians knew that Jesus would be trapped whether he said "yes" or "no." We know that God can't be put in a corner! Jesus was not fooled by the flattery. "But Jesus perceived their wickedness, and said, Why tempt ye me, ye hypocrites?" (v. 18). (Notice that both the political and religious sides were hypocritical.)

Today religion is the main enemy of Christianity. Christianity is not a religion. Christianity is a relationship between us and the Lord Jesus Christ. Religions are nothing more than Satan's counterfeit for Christianity.

Today in foreign countries people are starving to death in the name of religion, while food, cows which are considered holy, walk the street. Around the world, more people are dying and, (without knowing Jesus, going to hell) in the name of religion than anything else.

Elements which call themselves "the church," are really nothing more than religion which has joined itself with government to give us a unification of church and state. Religion has influenced the land against the Church of the Lord Jesus Christ.

Religion has presented entangling arguments which have caused the nation to listen less to God's Word. To continue moving in that direction would cause us to lose our freedoms. Ultimately Satan is trying to destroy our freedom to witness for the Lord Jesus Christ.

11

The Purpose of Government

Freedom to Spread the Gospel —

God gave us freedoms and designed government to protect those freedoms so that we can spread the gospel of the Lord Jesus Christ. By hearing God's Word and praying for our country, we can lead a quiet and peaceable life which will enable us to more easily spread the gospel.

First Timothy 2:1,2 states:

I exhort therefore, that, first of all, supplications, prayers, intercessions, and giving of thanks, be made for all men; For kings, and for all that are in authority; that we may lead a quiet and peaceable life in all godliness and honesty.

Satan and his forces are trying to ruin our quiet and peaceable life to stop us. He does not like Christians witnessing to people about Jesus and missionaries going to other countries; he does not like strong churches, and he does not like God's Word.

God gave us freedoms based upon the ability to exercise our free will. Man was created with a free will and has the freedom to accept or reject Jesus. Satan tries to work through or control governments to stop believers from spreading the gospel. But he is also trying to limit or eliminate men's freedom in order to stop them from using their free wills to accept Jesus.

God Himself has a will. Jesus said that He came to earth to do God's will. (John 5:30; Heb. 10:7.) The Holy Spirit came to do the will of the Lord Jesus. Jesus said, "...when he, the Spirit of truth" (*the Holy Spirit*), "is come, he will guide you into all truth: for he shall not speak of himself; but whatsoever he shall hear, that shall he speak..." (John 16:13). And, "...he shall testify of me" (John 15:26).

Jesus knew how important it was to do God's will. We read in Matthew, chapter 4, that when Jesus was in the wilderness and Satan came to tempt Him to go against God, Jesus made it clear three times that He was going to do the will of God. "It is written...," He said.

The strongest test of Jesus' will was in the Garden of Gethsemane shortly before He was crucified. He said, "O my Father, if it be possible, let this cup pass from me: nevertheless not as I will, but as thou wilt" (Matt. 26:39). No matter how strong the temptation was, Jesus "was in all points tempted like we as are, yet without sin" (Heb. 4:15). He always submitted Himself to the will of God. Therefore, when He went to the cross, He arose from the dead. (Phil. 2:7-11.) If we submit ourselves to God's will also, God will exalt us. (1 Pet. 5:6; James 4:6-8; Luke 14:11.)

When Adam came into this earth, he did not choose to accept God's will. Adam, of his own will, enslaved all of mankind. When Jesus came into this earth, of His own will, He freed all of mankind. Once we accept the plan of God by receiving Jesus, the Holy Spirit will guide us into God's will for our lives. (John 16:13.) When God designed government, He intended for leadership to guard individual freedoms so that citizens would have the freedom to accept or reject Jesus.

Freedom is not license. License says, "I can exercise my free will even to violate the free will of others." If your free will violates someone else's freedom, their rules and boundaries, then it is wrong. You cannot use your freedom to steal someone's private property or murder them. The purpose of government is to protect freedom — the exercise of our free wills and that of others.

Divine Institutions —

To protect our freedoms God instituted divine institutions for all men. The first one is marriage. With marriage comes commitment. A nation is held together by individual commitment. Marriage is the building block of all society, because as the home goes, the nation goes. From marriages cities are built, then counties, then states, then nations.

Satan has tried to destroy the home by attacking marriage. Through the trend of couples living together rather than marrying, Satan is attacking commitment. If the living arrangement does not work out, the two can just walk off and leave each other. Satan attacks the divine institution with sin. People who are "living together" are committing fornication. This is sin and will hurt and eventually destroy both members involved. (Prov. 5:11,22,23.) You cannot walk away from a relationship and think you will not be hurt. Fornication is one sin which comes against you own body. (1 Cor. 6:18.)

Second, God ordained family. God has ordained the family to train children in His ways. Ephesians 6:4 states: "And, ye fathers, provoke not your children to wrath: but bring them up in the nurture and admonition of the Lord." We saw earlier that the home is an incubator for a child to learn about authority.

Church programs should simply reinforce and extend what the child is learning at home. Satan is attacking the home with rampant divorce to place the children in a position in which he can infuse them with his knowledge.

There has been a sudden rise in the incidence of children being molested in day-care centers. Of course the people being employed in the centers need to be scrutinized more carefully, but why are so many children in day-care centers?

Many children are there for very good reasons. But many are there because Satan's attack on the family in the form of divorce has made it necessary. A woman may have to work to support herself and her children if her husband leaves her. Someone who wants to use his or her free will to dissolve his marriage is not using his freedom; he is taking license to infringe upon the free will of his partner. This is not right. God ordains marriage, not divorce.

A woman's highest priority, her calling, is to raise her children in the ways of the Lord. (1 Tim. 5:14; Titus 2:3-5.) The family is the incubator to bring up the next generations.

Third, God ordained nations. Movements toward one world government with one leader before the return of Jesus Christ are not of God. These movements will end when the Antichrist, the incarnation of Satan, will attempt to take the place of Jesus as the world's leader. (Zech. 11:15-17; Dan. 7:8; 9:27; 2 Thess. 2:3,4,8,9.) We saw that when the people tried to build their own monument, the tower of Babel, and forget about God, God destroyed it and separated them into nations and divided their languages. If corruption begins in a government, it usually spreads throughout the system. If strong independent countries exist and corruption breaks out, it is usually contained within its own national boundaries. The strong godly nations will continue following after God. Internationalism is another attempt by Satan to stop the preaching of the gospel.

Fourth, God ordained free enterprise, big business: the freedom of private business to operate for profit in a competitive system with a minimum of control by the government. Big business is a major strength of a country.

Throughout the Bible, we see examples of God condoning the business principles of free enterprise. For example in the parable of the talents, we see that the master was pleased with his servants who used the talents he gave them to gain more. (Matt. 25:14-30.) The man did not divide the returns equally among the servants.

The Bible says to work in order to have something to give to someone with a need. (Eph. 4:28.)

The Bible says, "Beloved, I wish above all things that thou mayest prosper and be in health, even as thy soul prospereth" (3 John 2). Today there is a resurgence in the message that God desires for His people to prosper so that more money can be given in offerings to further the spreading of the gospel.

Man's attempts to equalize by taking from the rich to give to the poor through higher taxing of higher incomes paves the way for socialism. The concept of socialism, the system of ownership by society rather than private individuals in which all members of the community share in the work and the goods, is not Biblically based. Socialism can eventually lead to communism, the system in which the state owns the goods and distributes them as needed. Communism suppresses all individual liberties which limits the preaching of the gospel.

In the name of equality and equity, freedoms are slowly being taken away. Definitely, everyone should have equal rights. We should not be discriminated against in the secular market on the basis of race, color, religion, sex, national origin, or age (although sin should not have an equal right with righteousness as in the case of homosexuality). We say that we are all born equal. To some extent that is true, and to some extent it is not. We should all have the same opportunities, but not everybody has the same mentality, ambitions, motives, or abilities.

Not everybody produces the same type or amount of work. Some people have a natural ability to make money; other people do not. There will always be blue collar and white collar workers; low, middle and upper class. Jesus commented that "...ye have the poor always with you..." (Matt. 26:11). The governments under socialism are trying to bring everyone to the same level. They are trying to take from those who have and give to those who have not — a chicken in every pot, the most good for the most people. Men try to produce equality when only God is capable. It has to be supernatural, a changing of man's heart, not his environment. If the wealth of the entire world were evenly distributed, within a few years the smart ones would have it all back and the others would lose it.

The only Kingdom in this earth where true equality exists is in Jesus' Kingdom. "There is neither Jew nor Greek, there is neither bond nor free, there is neither male nor female: for ye are all one in Christ Jesus" (Gal. 3:28). When we come into the Body of Christ, we are all truly one, made into the image of the Lord Jesus Christ on the inside of us. In the New Birth, we are seated with Jesus not in earthly places, but in the highest; in heavenly places. (Eph. 2:6.) God takes us right to the highest places.

True equality begins at the cross. But Satan uses the fight for equality in the world to continually stir up strife, to keep our eyes on a symptom rather than the cause of the disease. He tries in every way he can — under the guise of equality, in the name of human good — to tear down Christian values, to tear down the home and the Church so that he can bring in his kingdom.

Satan has attacked the divine institutions to destroy commitment, to encourage sin, to stop our children from learning the ways of the Lord, to stop the believers in a nation from uniting in prayer through his attempts to internationalize, and to stop believers from experiencing prosperity.

Why is Satan aiming at America to try to make us crumble? Why is he focusing his energy into international affairs to come against us? Why is he bringing communism to encroach on every side?

America is the primary source of sending the gospel message to the world. By aiming to destroy our freedoms, Satan is trying to tear down our quiet and peaceable life in order to ultimately destroy our nation and stop us from spreading the gospel. Today Christians in this country are rising up together against Satan. He has gone too far by encroaching on our right to preach the gospel!

Liberties —

What can we do legally to protect our freedoms? Use the liberties God has given us to protect them. Spread the gospel, pray and vote by our convictions.

To protect our ability to spread the gospel: pray for the leaders of our nation so that we can live a quiet and peaceable life. God wants all men to be saved and to come into the knowledge of the truth. (1 Tim. 2:4.) Pray that our leaders will become born again and come into the full knowledge of the truth of God's Word so that they will know how to preserve our freedoms.

12
Submission and Obedience

In an earlier chapter we saw that, according to Romans 13:1, every soul should be subject to the higher powers because the powers that be are ordained of God. The way that a person in authority handles the position may not be of God, but the position is of God.

We should never obey someone in authority without question, because the people in authority are not perfect! God gives authority to imperfect people because there are no perfect people!

In my opinion, God has asked us to pray for those in authority because they are imperfect. Only God, Jesus, and the Holy Spirit are perfect, and they do not need prayer! Jesus never prayed for God; God never prayed for Jesus.

Submission, an Attitude; Obedience, an Act —

There is a difference between submission and obedience. We can submit, but not obey. And when we disagree, we can do it in an agreeable manner.

Submission is not the same as obedience even though they are closely related. Submission is an attitude of the heart, a willingness. Isaiah 1:19 says, "If ye be willing and obedient, ye shall eat the good of the land." Obedience is an act: the verse says "and obedient."

Philippians 2:8 says of Jesus: "And being found in fashion as a man, he humbled himself, and became obedient unto death, even the death of the cross." When Jesus humbled Himself, He submitted to God's plan, *then* became obedient and went to the cross. According to First Timothy 2:1,2 we are to pray for people in authority so that we will have a quiet and peaceable life. To me this is saying that submission to authority brings a quiet and peaceable life.

Submission never brings bondage. Submission to Jesus brings freedom. Jesus said, "And ye shall know the truth, and the truth shall make you free" (John 8:32). Therefore, submission to authority should also bring freedom, because we are submitting to Jesus' authority.

Obedience without a submissive attitude is bondage and slavery. We can have a submissive attitude and still not be obedient. I would rather that someone who works for me be submissive and disobedient than be obedient without a submissive attitude. Someone who is obedient, but not submissive does what he is asked to do, but with a rebellious attitude, with bad feelings inside. He may talk behind your back. I would rather that someone comes to me with a submissive attitude and say, "I respect your position, but I disagree with what you have asked me to do."

God has asked the wife to be submissive to her husband, but not necessarily obedient. If a woman's husband wants her to go to a bar and drink with him, she would be violating her principles based on God's Word. If she said she would not go with him, she could still be submissive in her attitude, even though not obedient.

Disagreeing with Authority —

We may not agree with some of the things the authority says, teaches, or decides. But we must remember to respect the authority's position when we disagree. Rebellion against authority only brings down the wrath of God. There are ways of disagreeing in a respectful way.

We see in First Timothy that immediately before Paul states that people should pray for authorities, he gives the example of Hymenaeus and Alexander, two rebels against authority who did not understand proper submission. (1:19,20; 2:1,2.) Paul is encouraging people to pray for those in authority to avoid falling into the same trap that Hymenaeus and Alexander did.

First Timothy 1:18-20 states:

This charge I commit unto thee, son Timothy, according to the prophecies which went before on thee, that thou by them mightest war a good warfare;

Holding faith, and a good conscience; which some having put away concerning faith have made shipwreck:

Of whom is Hymenaeus and Alexander; whom I have delivered unto Satan, that they may learn not to blaspheme.

Hymenaeus Disagreed in Doctrine —

In Second Timothy 2:16-18 we read that Hymenaeus and another man, Philetus, were preaching a false doctrine that the resurrection of the saints had already come, and in doing so, they were overthrowing some people's faith. Hymenaeus was apparently called to the ministry, but disagreed on this point with Paul. Instead of discussing the matter with Paul, he tried to pull away from Paul's authority and prove his own doctrine.

Sometimes people put more value in the person preaching than in the Word being preached. This is unfortunate, because if the minister makes a mistake, people may leave the Lord. A minister may have a gift to teach, but he has to live what he teaches in the same way everyone else does. His teaching should direct the people to the Lord. A man may let you down, but Jesus said, "I will never leave thee, nor forsake thee" (Heb. 13:5). The people admired Paul, and when they saw the division in the ministry that Hymenaeus created, they were the ones who suffered.

Verses 14 and 16 state:

Of these things (*the promises of God*) put them in remembrance, charging them before the Lord that they strive not about words to no profit, but to the subverting of the hearers.

But shun profane and vain babblings: for they will increase unto more ungodliness.

There is nothing wrong with holding doctrines which differ from those of other people. In fact, we may discover that two different authorities; ministers, for example; may teach two different viewpoints on the same subject. We can never reach a point of perfection in God's Word on earth. Until we go to heaven, we will always be learning from God's Word. The problem comes when we rebel against authority by preaching the idea to people and striving about words, because we may subvert their faith, causing it to "shipwreck."

If we hear a pastor preach something we do not agree with; rather than telling other people our point of view, which would show that we think the pastor is wrong and cause division; we need to walk in love and study the subject in the Bible to search for the truth. Second Timothy 2:15 states: "Study" (*meaning "be diligent"*) "to shew thyself approved unto God, a workman that needeth not to be ashamed, rightly dividing the word of truth." After studying the Bible and praying, if we still believe we are right, we should talk to the pastor about the subject. If other pastors are like I am, we desire to hear good, honest criticism. But the person questioning the matter should discuss it without an attitude of rebellion.

Until we get to heaven we will disagree on different points. Instead of becoming an island to ourselves, we must flow together as members of the Body of Christ and talk out our differences — even if we never understand the other person's point of view — rather than bickering back and forth or letting division develop between ministries.

Alexander Disagreed Personally —

Two other verses mention Alexander (who I believe is the same Alexander Paul referred to in 1 Tim. 1:20). Paul said, "Alexander the coppersmith did me much evil: the Lord reward him according to his works: Of whom be thou ware also; for he hath greatly withstood our words" (2 Tim. 4:14,15). The Jews tried to use Alexander in a uprising against Paul (Acts 19:33).

Alexander despised Paul. It should not be this way, but sometimes people who dislike someone else will dislike everything about the person. In their eyes everything the person does is wrong. It seems that was the way Alexander was about Paul. Alexander rebelled against Paul because of a personal hatred for him.

There will be people we do not like as well as others. If we personally do not like a leader, again, we are to respect the position he holds and treat him with honor and love, because God created the position.

Employers —

Ephesians 6:5-8 states:

Servants, be obedient to them that are your masters according to the flesh, with fear and trembling, in singleness of your heart, as unto Christ;

Not with eyeservice, as menpleasers; but as the servants of Christ, doing the will of God from the heart;

With good will doing service, as to the Lord, and not to men:

Knowing that whatsoever good thing any man doeth, the same shall he receive of the Lord, whether he be bond or free.

When this passage was written, employees and employers were called servants and masters. Employees (servants) are to be obedient to their employers (masters) "according to the flesh." Notice that it does not say "according to the spirit." We are to listen to our employers and obey them on the job. They do not control our spiritual life.

We are to obey our employers "with fear and trembling." Mark 5:30,33 tells us that the woman who, after touching Jesus' garment, was healed from the issue of blood she had had for twelve years approached Jesus with "fearing and trembling" after He said, "Who touched my clothes?" Philippians 2:12 says, ". . .work out your own salvation with fear and trembling." We are to approach our employers in the same respectful way that we approach God. The way that we receive an earthly authority is the way that we receive the One Who is the ultimate authority.

Serve your employer in singleness of heart. Obey him as you would Jesus, the One over him. Work on your job not ". . .with eyeservice, as menpleasers. . ." giving your best whether your employer is there to see you or not. He may not always be there, but Jesus always is. Jesus, not man, is the source of your paycheck. If you are treated unfairly by your employer, the Lord will make it up to you some other way. Jacob worked for his uncle Laban for fourteen years and his wages were lowered ten times, but God rewarded Jacob for his submissive attitude. (Gen. 31:7,9.)

When you do your job as to the Lord, God will reward you. You can know that ". . .whatsoever good thing any man doeth, the same shall he receive of the Lord, whether he be bond or free." Only God can truly reward and promote.

Jesus said, ". . .ye shall receive power, after that the Holy Ghost is come upon you: and ye shall be witnesses unto me both in Jerusalem, and in all Judaea, and in Samaria, and unto the uttermost part of the earth" (Acts 1:8).

This verse does not say that we will receive power to *do* witnessing, but to *be* a witness. In other words, your actions can speak louder than your words. Yes, there are times to speak to spread the gospel, but not on company time. The way that you do your job is important. Sometimes believers share Jesus with others on company time, then are fired and think the reason is that they were "persecuted for righteousness' sake" (Matt. 5:10). That is not the reason. The way that you do your job is as much of a witness as what you say.

Your being the most productive person on the job and the most stable, while other people are fearing inflation, recession, and cutbacks, is as much of witness as *telling* people you are born again. People will beat a path to your door to find out why you are so stable. Their question will give you an excellent opportunity to say, "Jesus is in me, His Spirit is in me, and my needs are not supplied according to this company. My needs are supplied according to His riches in glory by Christ Jesus. I'm believing God that I won't be laid off, but even if I were, God would have a better job for me. He has many more channels to bless me. He's the Source."

In heaven you may see some member of your company whom you never dreamed would be there. Because you did your job as to the Lord, he was witnessed to by that. You had a part in his salvation that you never knew about. It was one of those small things that contributed to him receiving Jesus. Until we reach heaven we will not know all the effects our actions had to help bring people to salvation.

Go to God —

In disagreeing with an authority, instead of rebelling go directly to God. If you disagree with something the person in authority says or teaches or with his politics, or if he does something wrong, study the Scriptures on the subject, pray, then talk to the person, if necessary.

If the person in authority rubs you the wrong way, instead of talking about him to other people, pray for him. If he is a government leader who does not know the Lord, we know that God wants him saved and to come into a knowledge of the truth. (1 Tim. 2:4.)

The Bible says that the god of this world, Satan, has blinded the minds of unbelievers so that the light of the glorious gospel cannot shine into them. (2 Cor. 4:4.) You have a right to pray to stop the forces of Satan against unbelievers so that the light can shine in, and to pray that according to Luke 10:2 believers will cross their paths. The Lord of the harvest will send laborers to that government leader.

For someone who is a believer, pray that he will come into the full knowledge of the Lord and that the eyes of his understanding will be enlightened. (Eph. 1:17,18.) Also pray for yourself, that your eyes will be open to come into the full knowledge of the truth.

Those Who Despise Government —

Second Peter 2:9,10 states:

The Lord knoweth how to deliver the godly out of temptations, and to reserve the unjust unto the day of judgment to be punished:

But chiefly them that walk after the flesh in the lust of uncleanness, and despise government ["authority" AMP]. Presumptuous are they, selfwilled, they are not afraid to speak evil of dignities ["dignitaries (glorious ones)" AMP].

The Lord knows how to deliver the godly out of temptations, and to reserve for the sinner the judgment day to be punished, but the believers who are carnal, the ones who walk after the flesh, who despise government (authority), are presumptuous and self-willed. They are so arrogant, they are not even afraid to speak evil of leaders, earthly or heavenly.

These rebellious carnal Christians will not listen to God's Word; they will not listen to a minister. Second Peter 2:13 calls them "spots" and "blemishes"; Jude 8 calls them "filthy dreamers." And Second Peter states that they ". . .shall utterly perish in their own corruption; And shall receive the reward of unrighteousness. . ." (vv. 12,13) and "For it had been better for them not to have known the way of righteousness, than, after they have known it, to turn from the holy commandment delivered unto them" (v. 21).

In earlier chapters we saw the destructive results which come from not listening to God's Word. We have also seen that ". . .rebellion is as the sin of witchcraft. . ." (1 Sam. 15:23). From First Timothy 1:18-20, Second Peter 2:9,10,12,13, and Jude 8, we can understand how seriously God regards the importance of respecting authority. The stability of a nation can depend upon how well its people submit to authority, because "the powers that be are ordained of God." (Rom. 13:1.)

13

The Chain of Command in Governments and Churches

We have seen that we are to submit to and pray for those above us. God has established a chain of command with Him and His Word as the final authority. When we submit to and pray for the authority above us, the nation will be stable, because the authority of God is being recognized.

First Timothy 2:1 tells us to pray for "all men." The Greek word for *men* in this verse is *anthropos* which refers to all mankind. ("Anthropology" comes from this word.) Verse 2 pinpoints a specific type of man we are to pray for: "...kings, and for all that are in authority." "...kings" refers to authorities in government positions; "all that are in authority" refers to other kinds of authorities: in the Church, in the job, and at home.

Authorities in Government —

In America our modern-day equivalent of king is the President of the United States. Other civil authorities under the President are the Vice-President, congressmen, senators, governors, those people in the local levels of the state, the counties, and the districts — the mayor, policemen, firemen. We should pray for our policemen; our children should pray for their teachers and the principal of their school, to recognize authority.

Authorities in the Church —

First Timothy 2:7 refers to the authorities in the Church we are to pray for: the ministers. Paul was a minister. Paul said, "Whereunto I am ordained a preacher, and an apostle, (I speak the truth in Christ, and lie not;) a teacher of the Gentiles in faith and verity." "Whereunto" refers to the previous verse: testifying in due time of Jesus Who gave Himself as a ransom for all. ". . .verity" means "truth." Paul is saying he is ordained a preacher and apostle for the witness of the Lord Jesus and teaches the Gentiles in faith and truth. He is saying to pray for him.

We often see in the Bible that Paul asks for prayer that boldness would be given him as he declares God's Word and that while he is in bonds he can minister the gospel to those around him.

Ephesians 4:11,12 lists the fivefold ministry gifts. "And he gave some, apostles; and some, prophets; and some, evangelists; and some, pastors and teachers; For the perfecting of the saints, for the work of the ministry, for the edifying of the body of Christ." ". . .he" is Jesus. Jesus gave the ministry gifts to men.

Notice that verse 11 says "some." Some men — not everyone — are called to stand in these offices. If everyone were called to one of these offices, there would not be any people in the congregations! These ministry gifts have authority over us and are anointed to help perfect us. We may not always agree with their teaching, but we are to submit to them (in the way that we discussed in this book) and pray for them.

Responsibilities to the Authorities in Ministry —

The Bible gives us the obligations and responsibilities we are to have toward the ministry gifts.

First Thessalonians 5:12,13 tells us, "And we beseech you, brethren, to know them which labour among you, and are over you in the Lord, and admonish you; And to esteem them very highly in love for their work's sake. And be at peace among yourselves."

You may wonder how you can get to know your pastor if there are 500 people in your church. Paul had thousands under him. "Know" in this verse means "know about" rather than "become close friends with."

To "esteem them very highly in love" does not mean to put the authority on a pedestal as if he were perfect. It means to esteem the gift of God in him and his position, not worship him. It means to overlook his faults and pray for him.

We are to "esteem them. . . for their work's sake" (the sake of their production). Jesus said, ". . .the tree is known by his fruit" (Matt. 12:33). The passage ends, "And be at peace among yourselves."

First Timothy 5:17,18 says, "Let the elders that rule well be counted worthy of double honour, especially they who labour in the word and doctrine. For the scripture saith, Thou shalt not muzzle the ox that treadeth out the corn. And, The labourer is worthy of his reward." We should make sure that our ministers are not starving. They should have "adequate financial support" (AMP).

Hebrews 13:7 says, "Remember them which have the rule over you, who have spoken unto you the word of God: whose faith follow, considering the end of their conversation" (manner of life). We are not to examine the lives of the ministers and do what they do; we are to follow their faith and observe the end result of their manner of life.

Hebrews 13:17,18 states, "Obey them that have the rule over you," (*"your spiritual leaders"* AMP) "and submit yourselves: for they watch for your souls, as they that must give account, that they may do it with joy, and not with grief: for that is unprofitable for you. Pray for us: for we trust we have a good conscience, in all things willing to live honestly."

Again we see that we are to obey and submit to our spiritual leaders, and pray for them. They will give an account in heaven for our response to their leadership. We want that to be a joyous occasion, not grievous.

14

The Chain of Command in the Home

A nation is held together by homes in which the parents honor God's order of authority and train their children in the ways of the Lord — proper submission to authority. A nation's strength comes from parents who pray and teach their children how to pray.

Authorities in the Home —

Ephesians 5:22-25 shows us the chain of command in the home:

> Wives, submit yourselves unto your own husbands, as unto the Lord. For the husband is the head of the wife, even as Christ is the head of the church: and he is the saviour of the body.

> Therefore as the church is subject unto Christ, so let the wives be to their own husbands in every thing.

> Husbands, love your wives, even as Christ also loved the church, and gave himself for it.

In the home, wives are to be submitted to their husbands as to the Lord. The husband is the head of the wife, even as Christ is the Head of the Church. Husbands are to love their wives as Christ loved the Church. Children are to obey their parents. (Eph. 6:1.)

In continuing with the theme of honoring and respecting people in authority and praying for them, Paul says, "I will therefore that men pray every where, lifting up holy hands, without wrath and doubting" (1 Tim. 2:8).

The Greek word for *men* in this verse is not the same as the Greek word, *anthropos*, for *men* in verses 1 and 4, which we saw previously refers to all mankind: men, women, children, adults, servants, masters. God would have all men (mankind) to be saved. But in verse 8 the Greek word for *men* is *aner*, meaning individual men — a male, a husband. Verse 8 is actually saying, "I will (or desire) therefore that *husbands* pray every where, lifting up holy hands, without wrath and doubting."

In verse 8 Paul is still continuing the theme of authority, but this time in the home. Husbands are to set an example for their families by "lifting up holy hands, without wrath and doubting."

This does not mean that husbands should raise their hands and worship on their job or while driving down the freeway in their car. The context of the chapter deals with submissiveness to authority. The husbands are instructed to raise their hands as a symbol of *submission*, not as an act of praise and worship. "Holy hands" means an outward lifestyle of holiness before the world.

There is no such thing as a self-made man. Where would we be if our parents had not taken care of us? If they had not fed and clothed us we would have died. In school, where would we have been without our teachers to help us? All through life we constantly need help to arrive at certain goals and enable us to step out on our own. But even then, we will continue to need help — we are never self-made. We are nothing without the people to whom we submit — the people who take care of us and protect us.

First Timothy 1:8 means that men are willing to show their submission to the Lord when they are at work, on the street or the golf course. They want the world to know that they are not islands to themselves or self-made men. They know that what they are and what belongs to them came from the grace of God. They are to pray without wrath (unforgiveness) and doubting (lack of faith) because those two things will stop prayer from being answered.

God has placed husbands at the head of their families, but they are not the ultimate head, the final authority. They still answer to God. No matter where they are — with the family, on the job — the greatest thing they can do is show their reverence to Jesus. For husbands to give honor and creed to the Lord Jesus will not take away from their masculinity; it will enhance it. To admit their strength comes from the Lord will not mean that they are less of a leader, but more of a leader. Husbands are also to set an example for their families in how to respect and pray for those in authority.

Women are next in the chain of command. First Timothy 2:9-12 discusses women's submissiveness to authority.

> In like manner also, that women adorn themselves in modest apparel, with shamefacedness and sobriety; not with broided hair, or gold, or pearls, or costly array;

> But (which becometh women professing godliness) with good works.

> Let the woman learn in silence with all subjection.

> But I suffer a woman not to teach, not to usurp authority over the man, but to be in silence.

Wives are to dress with "sobriety," which means with discretion, in modest apparel. There is nothing wrong with wearing gold and jewelry, but it should be worn modestly. Wives should dress to enhance their husbands, not to draw attention to themselves. Their dress should tell the world that they are taken, not available. The husband's witness of submission is his holy lifestyle (hands). The wife's witness of submission is her modest dress before the world.

The woman should learn in silence with all submission and not teach or usurp authority over her husband. She should not study the Word with the idea of using it to correct her husband. Even more important than her dress, the wife's attitude of the heart is a testimony to the world of Jesus Christ. First Peter 3:4,5 tells us that a quiet and meek attitude toward the husband is an "adorning...which is not corruptible." Gold, silver and clothing will one day wear away, but spiritual adorning is eternal and speaks louder than natural dress.

Nothing is more unsightly than a wife who is contentious toward her husband. She is telling those around her that she rejects his authority and is going about to establish her own.

These scriptures are not saying that wives cannot teach in the home. Throughout Proverbs the woman is presented as the teacher in the home and the husband as the disciplinarian. They are saying that women should not use their teaching ability to usurp their husband's authority.

If a woman disagrees with her husband, she should handle the matter privately so that the children do not see splits in the leadership. They need to see unity in the home just as the members of the Body of Christ need to see unity among ministers. Divisions need to be handled privately. Unity comes through submission.

These verses in First Timothy teach that a woman should dress to please her husband, and admire and respect him.

Children, Obey Your Parents —

We have already seen the importance of instilling in children the promises of God's Word. When a difficult situation or trouble comes, God's Word will rise up inside them. Children must be instilled with the importance of authority, because as adults they will be the ones responsible for the stability of the nation. Let's examine some scriptures about training children.

Ephesians 6:1-4 states:

Children, obey your parents in the Lord: for this is right.

Honour thy father and mother; which is the first commandment with promise;

That it may be well with thee, and thou mayest live long on the earth.

And, ye fathers, provoke not your children to wrath: but bring them up in the nurture and admonition of the Lord.

Notice that wives are to submit, but children are to obey. (Eph. 5:22; 6:1.) Submission requires knowledge. Because children are not old enough to know how to submit, they are told to obey. As they grow, they gain more knowledge and begin to understand why they were taught to do certain things.

Honour in verse 2 means "to esteem highly." Children are to esteem highly their parents' position because God gave the parents that position and obey even if they do not know why. Parents are not perfect and should explain to their children that they make mistakes. A child should know that if his father makes a mistake it will not damage his ability to run the family. He is still to be honored as its head.

When a child honors his father and mother, God promises that "it may be well" with him and that he "mayest live long on the earth." God gives this twofold promise to children for obeying their parents. The word "well" (*eu* in the Greek) is actually a root of "prosperous." If children obey their parents, they will prosper and live a long time. This is the same twofold promise given to all believers who obey God's Word: "Beloved, I wish above all things that thou mayest prosper and be in health, even as thy soul prospereth" (3 John 2).

Fathers are to bring up children in the "nurture" (discipline) and "admonition" (instruction) of the Lord. Discipline should be backed with instruction and instruction with discipline. The two work together.

When I spank my children I explain to them that I am doing it because I want them to come back to the right way because I love them. I go over scripture with them so that they know that I am disciplining them on the basis of God's promises. I tell them I want them to be prosperous, that "it may be well" with them, and I want them to live long lives and enjoy every single day. I tell them someday they will appreciate it. Of course, they do not appreciate it at the time!

Hebrews 12:11 says, "Now no chastening for the present seemeth to be joyous, but grievous: nevertheless afterward it yieldeth the peaceable fruit of righteousness unto them which are exercised thereby."

Even though I never want to spank my children, I do it because spanking is the correct way to discipline them. Proverbs 22:6 says, "Train up a child in the way he should go: and when he is old, he will not depart from it." The verse does not say "teach" or "spank"; it says "train." "Train" means "show."

Children often cry when you discipline them. They often start to cry as soon as they see you are going to spank them. This makes you not want to spank them! Proverbs 19:18 says, "Chasten thy son while there is hope, and let not thy soul spare for his crying."

Somebody may wonder, "How can someone honestly say he loves his children and spank them?" Notice that Proverbs 13:24 says, "He that spareth his rod *hateth* his son:

but he that loveth him chasteneth him betimes" (diligently). Children need to be "chastened" often. They forget quickly. But then we forget quickly, too. How many times have we been disciplined by the Lord because we keep committing over and over the same mistake?

Proverbs 22:15 says, "Foolishness is bound in the heart of a child; but the rod of correction shall drive it far from him." A child can act very foolish until he is spanked. Afterwards his whole attitude changes. He becomes very teachable. The discipline yields the peaceable fruit of righteousness. (Heb. 12:11.)

Proverbs 23:13,14 says, "Withhold not correction from the child: for if thou beatest him with the rod, he shall not die. Thou shalt beat him with the rod, and shalt deliver his soul from hell." Disciplining a child is very important. By driving the foolishness from him, he will accept the Lord — his soul will be saved from hell.

Proverbs 29:15 says, "The rod and reproof give wisdom: but a child left to himself bringeth his mother to shame." A child who is not disciplined will bring his parents shame.

Notice that in a child the rod drives out foolishness and gives wisdom. Believers receive wisdom from God's Word which drives out foolishness. Until a child is old enough to comprehend God's Word, the rod replaces the Word in the child's life. The rod sets guidelines in his life as the Word will when he is older. A child needs external discipline until he receives Jesus as his Savior and has the Word as his internal discipline.

There is a great deal of child abuse today. Some of the above scriptures refer to beating. The Bible is not saying to beat children on the back, legs, arms, shoulders, or across the face. God designed one place on the human body with a lot of padding for the discipline of children. A spanking there will sting, but not physically harm. Knowing when to stop is also important. One or two swats should get the point across.

Ephesians 6:4 says for fathers not to provoke their children to wrath, and the second part of the verse tells how to avoid doing that: by bringing them up in the nurture and admonition of the Lord. In other words, a father will provoke his children to wrath if he disciplines them but does not tell them why he is doing it. If a child says, "Why did you do that?" and the father says, "Because I'm Daddy, because I'm an authority, that's why," that father will provoke his child to wrath, then to rebelliousness. That type of discipline will take the spirit out of the child. Colossians 3:21 says, "Fathers, provoke not your children to anger, lest they be discouraged."

Proverbs 29:17 says, "Correct thy son, and he shall give thee rest; yea, he shall give delight unto thy soul." When children are disciplined, they will bring their parents peace and happiness. They will have good manners and will be submissive and obedient to their parents and filled with respect. They will know and profess Jesus. Their parents will be proud to call them their own. And these children will grow up to be responsible believers who will join with other believers to humble themselves and pray for the nation, who will contribute to the nation's stability by respecting authority and praying for the people above them.

In discussing the proper chain of command in the home, we are seeing what makes a nation strong. When unity is in the homes, a nation cannot be conquered.

15

Authority Comes from Submitting

Matthew 8:5-10 tells us of the centurion who asked Jesus to heal his servant:

And when Jesus was entered into Capernaum, there came unto him a centurion, beseeching him,

And saying, Lord, my servant lieth at home sick of the palsy, grievously tormented.

And Jesus saith unto him, I will come and heal him.

The centurion answered and said, Lord, I am not worthy that thou shouldest come under my roof: but speak the word only, and my servant shall be healed.

For I am a man under authority, having soldiers under me: and I say to this man, Go, and he goeth; and to another, Come, and he cometh; and to my servant, Do this, and he doeth it.

When Jesus heard it, he marvelled, and said to them that followed, Verily I say unto you, I have not found so great faith, no, not in Israel.

Jesus said, "I have not found so great faith, no, not in Israel." The centurion's faith was great because he recognized authority. He knew that sickness was under authority to Jesus as men were under authority to him. He was under authority and had men under him. Authority and submission are like a sandwich. You may have someone under you, but you are under someone yourself.

Someone will *always* be in authority over us, because the *chief* authority is Jesus. The power to be in authority comes from learning to submit. A person will not know how to handle authority until he has learned how to handle submission. If you never learned to submit as an employee, you probably will not be a good employer.

Someone who is called to one of the fivefold ministry offices — apostle, prophet, evangelist, pastor, or teacher — first needs to learn to humble himself. He needs to sweep floors, teach a Sunday school class, and contribute in other ways around the church and learn how to submit to authority. Even when you are the pastor of a church, you still answer to higher authority — Jesus.

Jesus is the sum total of the fivefold ministry offices. His name is above every name. But He was not exalted to that position until He humbled Himself and became obedient even to the point of death on the cross. (Phil. 2:8.) Even when you reach a position of leadership, it is those in submission under you that gives you power for authority.

Know Your Master —

Isaiah 1:2,3 states:

Hear, O heavens, and give ear, O earth: for the Lord hath spoken, I have nourished and brought up children, and they have rebelled against me.

The ox knoweth his owner, and the ass his master's crib: but Israel doth not know, my people doth not consider.

Even though the ox and donkey are hardheaded creatures, the ox knows who its master is and the donkey knows where to go for its food. Israel, full of rebellion, knew neither.

Verse 4 states:

Ah sinful nation, a people laden with iniquity, a seed of evildoers, children that are corrupters: they have forsaken the Lord, they have provoked the Holy One of Israel unto anger, they are gone away backward.

Why should ye be stricken any more? ye will revolt more and more: the whole head is sick, and the whole heart faint.

This verse is saying that Israel had become so rebellious against God's authority and had reverted so far that for God to try to discipline them anymore was almost pointless. The more He disciplined them, the harder they became.

God was talking to Israel, believers who had reverted, not sinners. Today many believers have rebelled against authority. They want to be the master themselves; they do not want to go where the food (God's Word) is. What good is the salt of the earth when they are in rebellion, especially when so far in rebellion that the more God disciplines them, the harder they become? God wants to discipline them to bring them back in line with His Word so that they can once again become effective salt to help preserve the nation.

God has called us to hear His Word; to be disciplined by it; to know who our Master is and who is in authority over us; to submit to God, His Word, and those above us; to be guided by the Holy Spirit and do what God tells us; to pray for those in authority; and to be a protector of our nation. When we follow the order of authority, nothing will be able to destroy our nation.

16
Citizens of Two Worlds

There can be separation in unity. Even though church and state are joined together, they are separate. Even though a husband and wife are one, they are individuals. Even though we live on earth, we are citizens of two worlds.

Philippians 3:20 says, "For our conversation is in heaven; from whence also we look for the Saviour, the Lord Jesus Christ." The word *conversation* in the Greek means "citizenship." If you are born again, you are a citizen of two worlds: a physical world, your country, and a spiritual world, heaven.

When you were born into the earth, you were a citizen of the earth — in the world and of the world, under the god of this world, Satan, and his system. When you become born again, you change citizenships. Suddenly, you are *in* the world, but not *of* it.

The real you on the inside is called the spirit man, the inward man (2 Cor. 4:16), which will last forever. The body will not last forever. When people go to heaven, their body does not go with them. Because it is made of the elements of the earth, it will stay here. (But in heaven we will have another body. According to Phil. 3:21, "our vile body" will have been "fashioned like unto his" — Jesus' — "glorious body.")

The part of you that is a citizen of your country is only temporary. The eternal citizenship in heaven inside of you is permanent.

If you have to choose between the two, your heavenly citizenship comes first. As we have seen, this does not mean that you rebel against the things of the earth, but that you obey the higher law of heaven.

You are a citizen of your country, but your first allegiance is to God. Second Corinthians 5:20 says, "Now then we are ambassadors for Christ, as though God did beseech you by us." We are here from another country to represent our country of heaven.

American ambassadors are sent to countries all over the world. They are *in* that country, but not *of* it. An American ambassador would not violate the laws of a country he is visiting. In fact, to represent the goodness of his country, he would cooperate as fully as possible.

As ambassadors from heaven, to be good representatives of Jesus on earth, we must cooperate to abide by the laws of the land. As believers, we should be model citizens. We are of two separate worlds, but it is God's desire that we pull the two together. Matthew 6:10 says, "Thy kingdom come. Thy will be done in earth, as it is in heaven."

Romans 13:1-4 addresses all people, believers and unbelievers. Verses 5 through 10 address only believers and describe our responsibilities to the government:

Wherefore ye must needs be subject, not only for wrath, but also for conscience sake.

For for this cause pay ye tribute also: for they are God's ministers, attending continually upon this very thing.

Render therefore to all their dues: tribute to whom tribute is due; custom to whom custom; fear to whom fear; honour to whom honour.

Owe no man any thing, but to love one another: for he that loveth another hath fulfilled the law.

For this, Thou shalt not commit adultery, Thou shalt not kill, Thou shalt not steal, Thou shalt not bear false witness, Thou shalt not covet; and if there be any other commandment, it is briefly comprehended in this saying, namely, Thou shalt love thy neighbour as thyself.

Love worketh no ill to his neighbour: therefore love is the fulfilling of the law.

Verse 5 tells believers to be subject. We are to obey the laws of the land not because we fear them, but because we know to obey is right. Unbelievers are afraid. Many believers obey the law because they are afraid of the authorities.

A believer should not steal because his conscience tells him stealing is not right. He should not even have a desire to steal because of the power of the knowledge of God's Word in him. A believer would not want to rebel against the laws of the land anymore than he would want to rebel against God. Some unbelievers who walk into a store might desire to steal, but a fear of the consequences of breaking the law stops them.

Verse 6 tells us ". . . for this cause pay ye tribute also. . ." Believers should be in submission to the government, and pay their taxes, out of love and respect rather than fear.

Verse 7 says to render tribute and custom, taxes and tariffs, and honor to whom we owe them. When was the last time you wrote a letter to someone in government to thank him for a good decision he made?

In verse 8 we are told to owe no man any thing, but to love one another. The context of this verse is still honoring the government. We are to make sure that we pay our duties, tariffs, customs, and tributes, but there is one debt left over. We can never pay off the love debt.

". . .he that loveth another hath fulfilled the law" (v. 8). ". . .love is the fulfilling of the law" (v. 10). When we love one another, we fulfill the Old Testament law. Verse 9 lists adultery, killing, stealing, bearing false witness and coveting — these are the symptoms discussed in Hosea, chapter 4. We stop the symptoms of national disintegration by knowing God's Word, standing on it, and operating in love.

How do we keep God's and man's laws? By operating in love. When I operate in love, I do not violate laws. I do not commit adultery, kill, steal, bear false witness, or covet. Verses 9 and 10 emphasize that if there is any other commandment, it is briefly comprehended in saying, "Thou shalt love thy neighbor as thyself" and love does not work any ill against his neighbor; love is the fulfilling of the law.

How much more of a responsibility do we believers have than unbelievers to be submissive to and obey the laws of the land. But we do it for a much more powerful reason than fear. As ambassadors of the God Who created this earth, the universe, the governments around us, Who lives inside us, we do it out of love.

Conclusion

God has a plan. But Satan has a plan also: to counterfeit God's plan. At the same time Satan causes war, he wants to bring peace. Under the guise of human good, he will author a peace movement, using man's effort to try to bring about peace. This does not work.

The thing that frustrates Satan is the very thing he caused: the nature of the flesh. He tries to bring world peace through people, then people become angry at each other and start wars.

We can have individual peace now through the New Birth, but we will have true world peace only through the Prince of Peace, the Lord Jesus, when He comes back to rule the earth during the Millennium, His 1,000 year reign on earth following the Battle of Armageddon. The Bible tells us that Jesus will reign forever and ever. His Kingdom will be on earth and in heaven, and we will be forever under His rule. (Rev. 22:1-5.)

We have seen that hearing God's Word brings prosperity to a nation. When God's Word reigns in a country, knowledge of witty inventions comes in to bless people. Proverbs 8:12 says, "I wisdom dwell with prudence, and find out knowledge of witty inventions."

The greatest time of productivity and worldwide expansion in every field will occur when Jesus comes back to rule and reign on the earth, because the knowledge of God's Word will cover the earth as the waters cover the sea. (Is. 11:9.) But until then, God's Word — His wisdom and knowledge — can stabilize us in a world that is falling apart. Isaiah 33:6 says, "And wisdom and knowledge shall be the stability of thy times, and strength of salvation..."

Someone may say, "I've prayed for the country, for my city. Nothing seems to have improved. I see as much corruption today as there has always been."

Sometimes prayer is like sowing seed. Crops don't come up overnight.

Remember the promise God gives us in Second Chronicles 7:14: "If my people, which are called by my name, shall humble themselves, and pray, and seek my face, and turn from their wicked ways; then will I hear from heaven, and will forgive their sin, and will heal their land."

There are no self-made men. We are not islands to ourselves. We believers are all members of the Body of Christ who can unite in prayer, in the power of agreement, to bring tremendous results. (Matt. 18:19,20). When enough believers in a nation stand up and do what they know to do based on God's Word and pray, their nation is on the road to recovery. Praying for those in authority and for our nation will preserve our land.

Bob Yandian, Pastor of Grace Fellowship in Tulsa, Oklahoma, has an anointing and extensive teaching background that enables him to convey the uncompromised Word of God with an everyday practical clarity. Primarily, Bob ministers to students of the Word — fellow full-time ministers, congregational members, and Bible school students.

A graduate of Trinity Bible College, Bob studied under its director and founder, Charles Duncombe, a contemporary and companion of Smith Wigglesworth. Bob also studied Greek at Southwestern College in Oklahoma City.

In 1972 Bob began teaching regularly at Grace Fellowship where he was a founding member. In 1973 he began working for Kenneth Hagin Ministries as Tape Production Manager then, in 1977, for Rhema Bible Training Center as a teacher. Later he became Dean of Instructors. In 1980 he began pastoring Grace Fellowship.

Bob has taught and ministered throughout the United States and Canada, in South Africa, Guatemala, and the Philippines. He has spoken at numerous Full Gospel Businessmen's Fellowship International meetings; the

Greater Pittsburgh Charismatic Conference; Bill Basansky's 1981, 1982, and 1983 jubilees; Salt Lake Institute of Religion (Mormon); and hosted the Local Church Seminar at Grace Fellowship.